I0438332

The Mind Of A Cop

The Mind Of A Cop

What They Do, And Why They Do It

Scott Fielden

iUniverse, Inc.
New York   Bloomington

The Mind Of A Cop
What They Do, And Why They Do It

Copyright © 2009 by Scott Fielden

All rights reserved. No part of this book may be used or reproduced by any means, graphic, electronic, or mechanical, including photocopying, recording, taping or by any information storage retrieval system without the written permission of the publisher or author except in the case of brief quotations embodied in critical articles and reviews.

The views expressed herein do not necessarily reflect the policies and procedures of any law enforcement agency mentioned within the book.

Cover Photo: Designs by Jackie Fielden

iUniverse books may be ordered through booksellers or by contacting:

iUniverse
1663 Liberty Drive
Bloomington, IN 47403
www.iuniverse.com
1-800-Authors (1-800-288-4677)

Because of the dynamic nature of the Internet, any Web addresses or links contained in this book may have changed since publication and may no longer be valid. The views expressed in this work are solely those of the author and do not necessarily reflect the views of the publisher, and the publisher hereby disclaims any responsibility for them.

ISBN: 978-1-4401-8654-7 (sc)
ISBN: 978-1-4401-8655-4 (ebk)

Printed in the United States of America

iUniverse rev. date: 11/17/2009

"The only thing necessary for the triumph of evil is for good men to do nothing."

—Edmund Burke

CONTENTS

INTRODUCTION

Cops. Just mention the word and some people's brain cells will start firing like over-heated popcorn as they recall their own encounters with "the law." Though some of their memories may be accurate, others can be as close to reality as Dr. Seuss was to being a cardiac surgeon.

For instance, if they've had a traffic ticket recently, their grey matter may conjure up images of a bug-eyed ogre ripping off a citation and stuffing it into their palm with all the gentleness of a prostate exam.

Maybe they were stopped for DUI, and recall the officer as a ringmaster who forced them to perform acrobatic maneuvers on the side of the road like a downtrodden circus animal. *Step right up, ladies and gentlemen, and witness amazing feats of balance while this person stands on one leg, touches their nose and recites the alphabet, all while under the influence of a mind-altering substance...*

But if they were saved from a violent assault or pulled from a burning vehicle as smoke clouded their consciousness, their mind may generate images of angels clad in polyester appearing from nowhere, rescuing them moments before they became just another name in an obituary column.

Images can be deceiving. The word "cops" conveys an image—a mental picture often based on some personal encounter with law enforcement. The reality behind this image, of course, is the living, breathing soul who wears the uniform. Remove all their equipment and they're human beings, just like everyone else.

Human beings who shoulder more responsibility than most would ever dream of.

It's not a stretch to say your personal safety, along with the protection of your family and property rests in the hands of these armored strangers. But how comfortable are you in placing this responsibility—this blind trust—in people you don't know much about? And, in exchange for the safety and protection they offer, are you willing to accept the darker boundaries they must occasionally cross in order to provide it?

If those questions make you squirm a little, maybe it's time you got acquainted with some of society's troubleshooters. Beyond the generic title of *officer*, these people have names. They have lives. They'd also like to reveal some things to you about law enforcement…if you'll keep an open mind.

It's challenging to describe what it's like to be a cop to someone outside of law enforcement, just as it would be for a new mother to describe the childbirth process to someone who hasn't passed a seven-pound human through their body. But if an explanation isn't at least attempted, can anyone really appreciate what goes on in the delivery room, or out on the streets during patrol?

While this book contains a variety of "war stories" from police officers, you'll also be exposed to the facts behind these stories, which are often left out of police-reality television shows. The adrenaline rush that comes with a high-speed pursuit or raiding a crack house certainly makes good viewing, and for those in police work, the effects can be intoxicating. But what the edited segments of excitement on television don't reveal is the tremendous toll policing takes on some officers—the high divorce rates, depression, reduced life expectancy and stress-related health problems. As such, sometimes it's their own quest for survival, as much as it is the law, which influences a cop's actions and attitudes when dealing with the public.

Compiled from interviews with patrol officers, investigators and counselors, this book provides a realistic look at the complex world of those who protect and serve. Its goal is to provide a more

complete understanding of what life behind the badge is really like...
an informative, yet entertaining look at the total package.

Because the material presented within is only a sampling of the
hundreds of thousands of sworn officers across the nation, there will
always be those whose feedback would fall outside the consensus
of the thoughts expressed within the chapters. But if you grouped a
hundred officers together and asked for their responses to the issues
posed throughout the book, more often than not, a significant majority
would respond in a fashion similar to what has been written.

It's been said that every cop has their own personal reasons for
putting on the badge. I was reminded of this one summer afternoon
as I walked across a parking lot in uniform. A little girl, about four-
years-old, separated herself from her mother's grasp and trotted
towards me. Without saying a word, she tightly wrapped her small
arms around my leg. "She likes hugging police officers," her mother
explained. That simple act of kindness left me speechless. It also
reminded me what I was doing represented a righteous cause, though
it was often imperfect work performed by a flawed person.

I'd like to thank Heath Dingwell, Ph.D., a fellow writer and
professor of criminal justice, for his invaluable insight and assistance
in providing interview material for this book. I'd also like to extend
my appreciation to all the officers who agreed to be interviewed during
our compilation efforts, for this project would not have been possible
without their candid feedback. Some were comfortable in allowing the
publication of their names; others chose to remain anonymous because
of the sensitive nature of their comments. Each of these officers has
our utmost respect for the jobs they do, and for the personal risks they
encounter every time they roll onto a scene to answer a call.

Finally, what you are about to read may or may not contradict your
opinions regarding those who wear a badge for a living. I hope perhaps
it will do a little of both, for we live in a world full of contradictions.
Just take a look at rapper-turned-actor, Tracy Marrow, a.k.a. "Ice T."
In 1992, he was the lyricist with a band that released *Cop Killer*, an
obscenity-laced song which promoted the killing of police officers.

Today, he plays a cop on a successful television series.

If that makes sense, then maybe our world isn't such a confusing
place after all.

1

THE DRAWING POWER OF POLYESTER UNIFORMS

"When you tell someone you're a cop, you get one of two reactions. They think it's the greatest thing in the world, or they're standoffish from you."

When someone is diagnosed with a case of *protectiveservitis* (medical translation: an inflammation causing the protect and serve areas of the brain to swell), they'll often turn to the classified ads in search of law enforcement employment opportunities. If the newspaper they're thumbing through incorporates a full-disclosure policy, a hypothetical advertisement may read:

HELP WANTED: Law enforcement agency is seeking individuals willing to work for relatively low wages while assisting those who harbor an attitude of indifference, even outright hostility. Must be able to tolerate working in a dangerous environment and witnessing horrific events. Potential loss of life, limbs and/or personal property must be considered. Applicants must be self-motivated and able to accept the frustrations of fighting a war they'll never win. Retirement benefits may not be available since the average lifespan of our employees is significantly less than that of the general public. Nights, weekends and holiday shifts required. If you desire to risk it all for people who wouldn't invite you to a cookout even if you supplied the steaks, have we got a career for you! Now interviewing.

Given this job description, one question should come to mind: why would anyone who's not heavily medicated consider wearing a badge and gun for a living?

It sure isn't for the people they'll be dealing with—the addicts, thieves, molesters, murderers and other souls disconnected from humanity. In all likelihood, it's not for the opportunity to view the blood spilled at a traffic crash or to see the remains of someone's head after a close-range shotgun blast. It probably isn't for the chance to assume the combined roles of marriage counselor, social worker, psychologist, lawyer and nurse. People study for years to get certified in just one of these fields and get paid quite a bit more than the cop working several off-duty jobs to make ends meet.

And it's definitely not for all the times they'll walk into a business and some clown, trying to be funny, throws up their hands and yells, "Hey, I didn't do it, officer!"

"I know it sounds corny, but—"

If you ask a hundred cops why they got into law enforcement, a surprising number of them will begin their response with those exact words. The rest of the sentence often goes "I wanted to help others" or "it was an opportunity to make a difference with my life" and even "I wanted to make things inconvenient for the bad guys."

Whatever the motive, if your back door is being kicked in by a meth-head who's willing to steal and maim for their next high, you won't think any reason a cop joined the force is corny. The only thing important to you will be how quick an officer can get there.

When someone begins a career in law enforcement, they step into a world far different from the one everyone else lives in. On the surface, their jobs capture the interest and imagination like no other, which explains why numerous police reality shows proliferate television. In fact, one of the longest-running programs in history is "COPS," which has entertained the masses for over 20 years. How many other professions have had a camera crew filming their every move for primetime broadcast throughout two decades?

Being a cop means you'll experience the events others read about in the newspapers, see on the evening news or discuss between rounds at their favorite watering hole. It means you'll have the opportunity to permanently impact the lives of people you meet on a daily basis, often with the ability to choose whether that impact is positive or negative. And for the adrenaline junkies, being a cop is like having a free pass to Disneyland...you can ride all the attractions as many times as you like, without having to wait in line.

But it also means the welcome mat isn't rolled out by everyone you come in contact with.

"Everybody likes the firefighter, the rescue squad people because they all do good things when they come. But when law enforcement shows up, somebody may be going to jail, or at the very least, someone is probably going to be angry."
Lt. Randy Bowers, Carter County TN Sheriff's Dept.

"No one calls us to anniversaries, birthdays or to parties because they want to see us. They call us because it's gone bad. You're never called for the good things; you're always called for the crappy ones. The person who does want you there only does so because they can't control the situation anymore."
Anonymous

As kids, most of us acted out our fantasies of being a superhero. It really didn't matter if we had a cape and mask, or even what superhuman strengths we gave ourselves. The important thing was we had the power to protect the innocent—the little guy— while bravely putting a dent in crime. Truth be known, somewhere in the deep recesses of the consciousness, fragments of those childhood superhero desires still exist within many adults. This may be why some of the most popular movies over the past few years have been about superhuman characters (with very human flaws), who wear attention-grabbing attire while fighting crime and protecting civilization from evil.

Substitute mortal abilities in place of superhuman powers and what have you got? A street cop.

If you rub elbows with enough officers, a couple of things will quickly become apparent. For instance, they don't possess any phenomenal powers, like the ability to hear a cockroach sneeze at forty yards. Also, they didn't join the force to someday have a highway named after them, their likeness molded into a bobble-head doll, or for people to sit around a campfire singing songs of admiration about their deeds. And they're not magicians—they can't snap their fingers and turn a high-crime area into Mr. Roger's neighborhood, no matter what training and tools you give them.

What they tend to be, however, are everyday folks from all walks of life who viewed police work as both an interesting and secure job, and who desired an opportunity to add value to their own lives by doing something for society.

"I think the public has a misconception about the police. Anybody who has ever had any long-term contact with us, like the chaplains, they had a perception of what the police were like. They were nervous to come to work here. It was like, 'I see all the stuff on television and wonder if they're really like that. I'm finding out—*geez* —they're real people. Everyday people. It's like going to my accountant. They're as nice as the people sitting there and you can talk with them about things.'

People somehow seem to think that the police—I don't know if they think we hire them from Mars—are so different from everyone else. They're not. I'm concerned about what I read in the paper about what's going on around the world and the environment. I've got bills to pay and cars to fix and have to feed my family. I've got exactly the same fears and concerns they have. We're really no different. For some reason this uniform makes it look like we're from a different species."

Lt. Karl Fisher, Eau Claire WI Police Dept.

Trying to understand all the motivations behind someone's decision to enter law enforcement can be as difficult as comprehending all those miscellaneous charges on your phone bill. Still, there's a common thread linking most responses, and it relates back to the familiar words stenciled across police vehicles everywhere—to protect and to serve.

According to a 2003 internet survey by POLICE magazine, 54% of the respondents stated that providing help to people was their primary motive for pursuing a career in law enforcement. Another 23% cited "putting the bad guys away" as their reason, followed by 15% who replied that enforcing the law is what lured them into the profession. The remaining 8% joined in order to pay their bills.

When considering some of the explanations from officers regarding their career choice, it doesn't take a seasoned detective to notice a familiar pattern emerges. Despite different personalities, gender, education and ethnicity, much of their feedback ultimately centers on similar thoughts.

"I decided on law enforcement because it's a noble profession, where you actually do something about the evils in our society instead of talking about it and relying on others. The entertainment value is fairly high and I didn't think I'd get as much satisfaction making other people money in the business world."

Sgt. Aaron Davis, Albany OR Police Dept.

"I became a cop for probably the same reason 90% of the people get into it; I wanted to help others. As time goes on, officers may become more cynical about that, but the initial reason most get into it is to help people. Every now and then things come up and that gets a little clouded, so you have to turn around and get refocused. You try not to lose sight of the main goal, and the ultimate goal is helping people."

Anonymous

"I was working as a food broker and wasn't really happy doing that. I was making good money, but to me, marking turkey wieners up two cents to make a profit—well, I just didn't feel like I was doing anything that was really worthwhile in society. There didn't seem to be any value with what I was doing. On a whim I took the cadet test and I ended up scoring in the top percentile and was hired. From the minute that I did it, I loved it. It was in my blood."

Capt. Mike Martin, Minneapolis MN Police Dept.

"Whether any cop wants to admit it or not, you come into the job because you want to make a difference. You want to contribute something to society, your country, your city or whatever. It may also have something to do with the adrenaline. Some people do it for the uniform, the perceived power or the status. It certainly isn't for the pay. The bottom line is that we're people just like everyone else. Not any smarter, not any tougher. Cops do tend to be creative problem solvers, however, since they're called upon to deal with the problems of others at the spur of the moment."

Anonymous

"I think everybody goes in thinking they're going to make a difference. Now, I didn't come in here thinking I was going to save the world, because I knew that wasn't a reachable goal. But I knew that if you worked hard and did things sufficiently, you could make a difference somewhere down the road. It may be a small, minute difference, but it's still a difference. If you ever get out of that mindset, it's time to hang it up."

Detective Sgt. Beth Dyke, Greeneville TN Police Dept.

"Many cops seem to be predisposed to enter law enforcement. It may be something that's been in the family for generations. Unfortunately, some are rather judgmental, and have no problem defining social and behavioral boundaries for others. Some are attracted to the excitement of the badge and gun, and others are attracted socially to the working environment.

I was originally an architect major in college, but the long hours hidden away drawing some insignificant attachment of some sort meant that I would be socially isolated, and I knew that I enjoyed working with and around people.

One day on my way home from class, I passed a police cruiser going the other direction. It was a sunny afternoon; the cop had his window down, his elbow extended and relaxed, his right hand lazily flopped over the steering wheel. He appeared to have found his niche. I immediately knew I wanted his job. To be outside, interacting with society, challenged by the knowledge it took to do the job and challenged by the job itself. That was all it took. The more I studied criminal justice, the more I enjoyed it. It's been an exciting and rewarding 24 years."

Sgt. Dave Cropp, Sacramento CA Police Dept.

Along with the self-satisfaction derived from the job, many officers feel working in an outside environment where your boss isn't constantly staring at you from the next cubicle is a key benefit, as is the variety of the job itself. Street patrol is pregnant with possibilities; each day delivers something new and anything can happen in an eye-blink. One moment you might be playing cowboy, trying to coax 900 pounds of quivering beefsteak off a county road and back into a pasture, and the next, you could be wrestling an armed felon to the ground, removing from their mind any thought that going to jail was an option they could simply decline.

"Talk to any cop and they'll tell you the streets are where it's at. The next call that comes over the radio, you have no idea what you're going to get involved with. Every day is something a little different. There's a part of me that would love to tear off these stripes and go back to the street. It would be fun to go back to my first two or three years and be out on the streets again—not as a supervisor, but as a street cop. One minute you may be involved in a chase, and the next you may be getting a cup of coffee, and then be involved in a shooting or a fight.

I've had my uniform shirt torn, glasses broken, even got pushed down a flight of stairs one time and thought I was paralyzed. I wouldn't trade all that stuff for anything. I wouldn't want to live it again, but to do the job, sometimes you have to get your hands dirty."

Sgt. John Holthusen, Minneapolis MN Police Dept.

Being known as someone can restore sanity to an insane situation—serving as the "go-to" person when needed—is also something which draws people into the fold. After all, the buck stops with the police; they don't have the option of calling 911. They can't say they'll come back when things are safer, can never call a draw or ask for a time-out. Regardless of the situation when they roll up to a scene, they have to deal with whatever presents itself, even if it's the street equivalent of wading knee deep in alligators hungry enough to commence the death roll.

"If you're able to effectively operate and do a good job in a situation where other people would never be able to do it, it brings you a sense of pride. Also, we know people appreciate the fact there are those who can take care of business when it needs to be taken care of. There's this saying in law enforcement that when the shots are fired, cops run towards it while everyone else is running away. To be one of the people who's willing to go there and take it on should give someone a sense of pride."

Capt. Mike Martin, Minneapolis MN Police Dept.

Do some people get into law enforcement for the ego gratification in wearing a badge and gun? Of course, but that's not necessarily a bad thing—as long as it's not the predominant reason they put the gear on. Truth is, a little bit of ego, along with self-confidence and a strong presence are assets in police work, as it's not an arena the meek thrive in. If you need convincing, just put on a uniform and walk into some seedy "bar and beer nuts" tavern. Pick out the biggest and loudest man-beast (which is usually someone who doesn't like being told what to do by the police) and politely ask him to sit down and behave so everyone else can enjoy their beverages. Upon regaining consciousness, you'll have learned an important lesson: it takes more than a cordial request to enforce the law with a select group of people.

"As a cop, I believe you need two personalities to survive; one for work and one for home. Your personal relationships can't survive having the same personality at home that you have at work. No one would put up with that. On the job, you have to be fearless and believe you can handle anything. This is one of those few jobs were you can't call a time out and say, 'I'll come back later.' When you get into a situation, you must control it. If you don't, you or your partner could die. You have to work through the fear and deal with what's in front of you right now. Society demands this.

To survive, you put up a safety zone around you and pray no one gets through it. You're on edge and ready. We require a lot from our officers and the expectations are very high. It's very hard to shut this off when you go home."

Sgt. John Holthusen, Minneapolis MN Police Dept.

Even after their leather gear becomes worn and the once exciting events become routine, law enforcement remains an addictive occupation for many officers. Whether it's the power and responsibility reflecting off the badge, the Valium-like calming effect the uniform has on those seeking refuge, the adrenaline rush of a hot call or simply the act of making a positive difference in someone's life, a lot of cops admit they can't imagine doing anything else for a living. In fact, 80% of the officers surveyed would recommend police work as a career choice, according to a 2003 web poll by POLICE magazine.

Before leaving this subject, there's another reason for entering law enforcement that's seldom mentioned, even though it's one the public may relate to most of all. And given the popularity of police reality shows, it should come as no surprise.

Being a cop means you have the best stories to tell at a party.

*

My partner and I were at the Detention Center when our sergeant brought the guy in. His name was Tony, and he was about as drunk and dirty as they came. He was a homeless guy, about 30-years-old, who'd been on the losing end of a fight. In the process, he'd also lost one of his shoes. Because he was complaining about his ribs hurting, we were told to take him to the hospital for evaluation.

For a reason I'll never know, on the ride to the hospital he became convinced that I was his uncle, who he loved very much. He was also sure I was running for president, and he was proud to be related to me. Who was I to tell him different? When a belligerent drunk bonds with you for whatever reason, you sometimes go with it. It helps keeps them calm.

My partner and I played off Tony's "relationship" with me while we waited in the exam room of the ER. Whenever he started getting loud and running his mouth, we'd remind him that he shouldn't embarrass his uncle, who was going to be president. It was either that, or we were going to end up wrestling him in front of everybody in the ER.

While he was stretched out on the gurney, he asked me to come closer to him. He said there was something important he had to tell me. My partner edged closer, in case he was going to come up off the bed. I walked over to Tony and he looked at me very seriously, saying he had to whisper what he needed to tell me. He wasn't a threat at the time, so I leaned over and kind of tilted my head so he could whisper whatever he had to say. Before I knew what was happening, he put his hand on the back of my head, rose up half-way, and planted a soggy kiss on my cheek.

"I love you, uncle," he grinned.

I was shocked. I could feel my face immediately turning red. My partner, standing across the bed, was wide-eyed and trying his best to keep from laughing. My first thought was to wash my face. My second thought was making sure he wasn't going to ride me about this for the rest of my life. I'd been riding him about letting a female abuse victim step in close and show him how her husband had smacked her on the forehead, which caught him completely off guard. And now here I was, leaving myself open for this.

After his exam, the three of us left the hospital. We couldn't transport Tony to a homeless shelter because he was still intoxicated. Faced with having to release him back into the cold winter night, we were concerned about him making do with only one shoe on. It was the end of our shift and we were being called back to the Detention Center, so we loaded him in the cruiser and headed down the highway. About a mile down the road, we decided to make a detour.

We pulled into the parking lot of a Dollar Store and took Tony inside. He got real quite when he saw what we were up to. We went to the shoe section and picked out a new pair of tennis shoes his size. When we walked up to the counter to pay for them, an older lady followed us to the cashier with the old beat-up shoe Tony had tossed aside back in the aisle.

"Young man, I think you left this behind," she said.

"No ma'am, I don't need that one now. It has bad memories. I got me some new shoes," he proudly replied.

After paying for the shoes, I went next door and bought him a pack of cigarettes and lighter. My partner and I then gave him $10 so he could buy himself something to eat. He thanked us from the bottom of his heart, hugged us both and promised to take better care of himself. We left him in the parking lot and made our way back to the Detention Center.

About four weeks later a news brief about Tony was in the local paper. He'd broken into a soft-drink truck and took several items, including a money bag that was left in the truck. A city officer found Tony in an abandoned house where he'd taken up residence without permission of the owner. He was charged with auto burglary and trespassing.

In the end, it seemed our help was a temporary relief for him at best. But that's not the point. In this business, you have to at least try to help people so that they will take the next step to help themselves. It's why I became a cop in the first place—to help people.

Besides, there are certain responsibilities that go along with being someone's uncle, even when you're busy running for president.

Ofc. Jerry Bennett, Washington County TN Sheriff's Office

*

The call came in as a fight in progress. When I got there, a young guy, maybe in his twenties, was standing in the middle of the road. I got out of my cruiser and started walking towards him. It was dark, so it took me several steps before I was close enough to see he was holding a knife in each hand. I immediately stopped and yelled for him to drop them two, maybe three times. He didn't, so I pulled my gun and took aim in case he rushed towards me. I yelled again for him to drop the knives.

The guy just looked at me and shook his head. "No way. Forget it, man. You'll just have to kill me!"

Well, I didn't want to kill the guy and told him that. He stood still for a few seconds, kind of acting like he was re-thinking his situation. "Either you shoot me or I'll kill myself," he finally said. He took a step back and put the knives up to his throat.

I'd never been in a situation where somebody was threatening suicide right in front of me. I didn't know how serious he was about doing it, or even if he was going to force me to do something I'd regret. All I could think of was to try and calm him down, to buy some time to figure a way out of the situation for both of us. Since he was far enough away where he didn't present an immediate threat to me, I took a chance on the first thing that popped into my mind.

He looked surprised when I put my gun back in its holster. He was even more surprised when I came up with the OC spray, stepped forward and squirted a stream right into his face. He dropped the knives, grabbed his eyes and took off running in the opposite direction. I chased him a short distance and tackled him in a ditch next to the road. He didn't put up much of a fight while I cuffed him. I think I wound up charging him with domestic violence and maybe also resisting arrest.

Because of his suicide threats, the court ordered him to be admitted to a psychiatric hospital. I kind of wondered what happened to him for awhile, but as time went by, I pretty much forgot about the incident.

A couple of years later a guy walked up to me in a grocery store when I was off duty. He smiled and said, "Mr. Rhudy, I just wanna tell you how much I appreciate what you did for me awhile back. You probably don't remember me, do you?"

I said no, but knew he looked familiar. Just couldn't place him.

He continued talking, and then I remembered he was the suicidal guy with the knives I arrested.

"You could've killed me that night, but you let me live instead," he said. "Because of you, I've turned my life around. I've got a family now, go to church and have become a better person. Thank you, Mr. Rhudy."

Whenever someone asks me if I've ever really made a difference on the job, I remember that guy. Makes be proud to be a cop.

Lt. Danny Rhudy, Washington County TN Sheriff's Office

*

I think it's the occasional "thank-you" and the appreciation you get from people that make the job worthwhile. You have to remember those things when the bad stuff happens, because the bad stuff probably outweighs the good stuff at least ten to one.

I've had the opportunity to save lives a couple of times, which is a highlight. One time, there was an elderly gentleman who was driving right next to the Target Center. He had a heart attack and rear-ended the car in front of him. I just happened to be driving by and got flagged down. I was able to pull him out onto the ground and do CPR on him and get him breathing again.

The interesting thing is he and his wife were in town visiting from somewhere else in the state, so his wife went with him in the ambulance to the hospital. I got with another officer and we drove his car over to the hospital and parked it there so they would have it when needed. Two hours later I'm inside the hospital, talking to the guy. How many other people work in a job where they can save someone's life and have the person thank them? I think that's a highlight of this job.

Capt. Mike Martin, Minneapolis MN Police Dept.

*

Typically, you get informants to tell you where the drug houses are. We got a complaint that some people were dealing drugs; a lot of activity was going on around their house. We knock on the door to talk with them, not knowing what we'd find. Well, this dumbass opens the door, and there's crack right there in plain view. Some of the people inside started running, so right away I try and grab somebody. This one guy is kinda resisting and starts fighting with me. I took him by the throat and pushed him up against the wall, and his head went through the sheetrock. I was able to cuff him pretty easily after that.

About a year later, I saw the same guy in a homeless shelter/detox facility, one of the places where people try to improve their lives. I didn't remember him at first, but he came up and thanked me for doing what I did to him, because it got him off crack. Then I remembered the long conversation I had with him after putting his head through the sheetrock. I was pretty firm and talked about him being a damn idiot and that he was going to get his ass killed if he kept on that way.

And so a year later he's thanking me for all that. That was pretty cool.

Anonymous

*

There's always going to be some cases you look back on and say to yourself, "I'm glad I became a cop. I've had a positive impact in someone's life."

There was this family who lived next door to an elderly couple in their seventies. After the two families had gotten to know each other, the older couple assumed the role of surrogate grandparents to their neighbor's children. You know, kids sometimes wander next door to their neighbor's house to help water the garden, pick strawberries and things like that. Over time the parents became very trusting of their elderly neighbors.

Well, the older woman next door became ill and went through a debilitating disease, so the kids would go over there to comfort her. Just by being there, the kids would brighten up her day. Eventually the lady died, but the kids continued to bond with her husband. Unfortunately, he took advantage of the situation. He began fondling one of the children—a seven-year-old girl—kissing her on the mouth and things like that. The child knew something wasn't right. One day when her mother asked why her face was so red, the child told her what had been going on. Turned out the redness was caused by the rough whiskers of the elderly man.

Of course when the child tells her mother, the mother gasps in horror, so the kid just shuts down. When someone expresses "shock and awe" at kids in situations like that, they just shut down. The parents did the right thing and notified the police department and the Department of Children's Services. During this time, her father went to confront the neighbor, who, of course, denied doing anything. He puts the blame back on the parents, saying they should probably take the kid to a doctor. When I went to interview him, he did wind up confessing to what he had done, but attempted to explain it away. In fact, he had gone next door to the girl's parents and offered money to pay for the kid's college in order to settle the matter.

I knew he didn't just start abusing kids at the age of 75. In preparation for the trial, I went back further into his life and interviewed people in places where he'd previously lived and was able to find other victims of his predatory behavior. In the meantime, the girl and her family went through counseling and fortunately resolved much of the emotional damage related to the abuse. We were able to catch it in time before it escalated into something worse.

To this day, I feel I made a difference in the lives of the child and her parents because I was able to help stop the abuse before it escalated. It's been a success story, since I've been able to keep the abuser in prison. I've gone to parole hearings where he's used the "I'm an old man" routine and should be let out. But I knew he would likely commit the same type of behavior again if he were released.

Parents tend to let their guard down around people like that. They automatically think their kids may be okay around certain people, but there's no set standard of who's the perpetrator out there. They may seem to be the nicest guy in the world and that's why they appeal to kids. Those kinds of people know how to get their victims.

When you can stop abusive behavior and change a child's life, that's the ultimate. You've made a positive difference. That's why I got into law enforcement.

Detective Sgt. Beth Dyke, Greeneville TN Police Dept.

*

My experience with law enforcement began a decade and a half before I ever pinned a badge to my chest. My friend's father, John Klem, was a deputy sheriff with Forrest County, Mississippi, and was my first real experience with the professional side of law enforcement.

John Klem was a cop who was cool. He'd owned fast cars in his youth, didn't abuse the power behind his badge, made jokes all the time and would take his son James and I out to eat at the local Dairy Queen during his lunch break, where he would tell us humorous law enforcement stories with the skill of the best orators. My experiences with John dispelled all of the stereotypes and preconceived notions I ever had about law enforcement personnel. He was a Baptist reverend with his own church and congregation, possessed a very deep set of religious beliefs which he helped pass on to me at an impressionable age, and had a loving wife and three sons.

I fondly remember stuff like the time James and I were riding with his dad in the sheriff's unit and he had the CB radio tuned to Channel 19, where most of the radio traffic was. We were heading down the highway going to lunch when a trucker called out over the radio, "Breaker one-nine for a Smokey report."

Deputy Klem reached up, got the mike and calmly said, "You've got a Smokey, what do you need to report?"

John was always like that, having fun in life and making people around him laugh. It was his way of using his mind instead of his muscles and it worked wonderfully. He made it easy for people to like him; his jovial nature put off a lot of confrontations that would normally come from those who were suddenly in the presence of a law enforcement officer. That's what I remember most about that incredible man, but then again, it's all I have left now—fond memories.

He died in the line of duty in 1985.

I remember that day well. John had arrested a repeat loser earlier that week, one he was more than familiar with. After being released on bond, the suspect headed to the Big K Truck Stop on US 49 North and started trouble with everyone there. John was patrolling that day and responded to the disturbance call. When he arrived on scene, a fight ensued between him and the suspect. Deputy Klem was tackled to the ground, had his .357 service revolver wrestled away, then was shot twice in the chest at point blank range with his own weapon. The suspect quickly fled, leaving John bleeding on the cold tile floor of the Mississippi truck stop.

Law enforcement officers are shot more often than people would like to admit, and only when it happens to someone close to you do you really stop and think about the sacrifices and contributions made by those who serve in the law enforcement community. John survived the initial attack and the suspect was later apprehended and held without bond. Emergency surgery at Forrest General Hospital in Hattiesburg stabilized John's life, but he had a bullet lodged against his spine that would leave him paralyzed from the waist down for the rest of his life. Other than the paralysis, the prognosis was guarded but optimistic. Two high-powered .357 rounds fired at point blank range can do a lot of damage to the human body. Don't let anyone ever tell you different.

While hospitalized, John accepted visitors with his usual cheerfulness and humor, though he was somewhat subdued due to his physical condition. Even after taking two magnum rounds, he still acted like everything was going to be fine, such was the power of his faith and character. John remained strong for everyone around him, especially his family.

I remember visiting John and seeing him lying in the hospital bed. He was still the greatest law enforcement officer I had ever known. Even with two gaping wounds punched through him and having more stitches than you'd see in a bad horror movie, he still had the positive attitude that I looked up to and admired. It looked like he would recover from his wounds; the doctors were optimistic that with therapy, John could get back a great portion of his life. We all began to hope for the best, but it was not to be.

John Klem died unexpectedly during the middle of the night, nearly a week after being shot. The official report was heart failure due to a blood clot arising from all the surgery and medications. There was nothing they could have done to save him.

And just like that, one of the greatest men I'd ever known was gone.

His funeral was one of the toughest things I've ever gone through in my life. Each shot from the twenty-one gun salute made me cringe with hate for the human animal that had taken away my friend's father. I felt a tear forming when the two officers rolled up the flag, folded it into a triangle, and handed it to John's widow. Something was torn from my life that day, and it left a hole in my soul that I could never replace. From that day forward, I vowed that if I could do anything to keep human animals off the street, like the one that shot Reverend/Deputy Sheriff Klem, then I would do everything in my power to do so.

When the City of Columbia sponsored their first reserve officer training program in 2000, I got that chance. After six months of training, which was held during nights and weekends, those completing the program would be sworn in as police officers for the city. There was no pay involved, other than being able to hire yourself out to local businesses for security work. It was never about money in the first place. Instead, it was because I believed one person can make a difference, and a team of strong-willed people who answer the call of duty can make a world of difference. I wanted to be a part of that team, and so I enrolled in the program.

Twenty-six long weeks of classroom studies, physical endurance tests, driving certifications, firearms qualifications, hand-to-hand combat and other law enforcement training left me stronger than when I'd started. I threw myself into the program, and when I graduated in June of 2000, it was one of the proudest moments in my life.

As a reserve officer, I'm subject to call up when extra personnel are required and remain on call 24/7/365. I wear the same badge, write the same tickets, drive the same Interceptor, chase the same criminals, and put my life on the line same as the full-time officers. The only difference is that I get to make my own hours and I don't draw a paycheck. It's all volunteer service.

Some say you'd have to be insane to want to do what a police officer does everyday—to put up with the insults, the abuse and the danger. In a society where criminals have more rights than their victims, where financial happiness is as close as a toll-free phone call to a lawyer, you'd have to be crazy to ever want to be a police officer, let alone do it for zero pay.

Crazy? Or maybe, just maybe, unselfish?

I'm willing to give my spare time and talents to the community so it will be a better place to live for my family and neighbors. I joined the Columbia Police Department because I wanted to carry on the same dream that John Klem once had. I wanted to answer the same calling he heard, to contribute what I could to making that dream a reality. I've always wanted to make a difference with my life, to use what God has freely given me in order to better the lives of others. Too many people never live up to their potential; they never realize what talents and gifts they have, or they simply fail to use them in any meaningful way. I didn't want to fall into that kind of lethargic lifestyle.

A lot of people don't understand what I do or why I do it, but I know John Klem would have understood. He would have approved of my decision and been proud of the things I've accomplished as a law enforcement officer.

And despite the people who still refer to us as pigs, I believe I became a police officer for all the right reasons.

Ofc. Christopher T. Shields, Columbia MS Police Dept.

2

FROM THE TRAINING ACADEMY TO THE STREETS

"The easiest thing to do in police work is to get yourself killed. Anyone can do that. It takes a lot of effort to stay alive and mentally sound on this job while trying to make a dent in all the mess that's out there."

If you're nurturing some warm fuzzy feelings about protecting and serving after reading the previous chapter, congratulations. Now you're familiar with the mindset many new recruits have when they first step onto the grounds of the training academy.

Some years ago, the primary focus of the academy was teaching the bread and butter fundamentals of law enforcement—what the laws are and how to arrest people, or the "bust 'em and book 'em" approach. Simple training for simpler times, grizzled veterans recall. Nowadays, the training program is much more extensive and is comparable to college course work. Hundreds of hours are devoted to classes ranging from administrative tasks to zone patrol, with the ultimate objective being the transformation of the rawest recruit into a functional officer.

It's during the academy training, which lasts from three to six months, that some of the preconceived notions of law enforcement give way to a more realistic view of what life behind the badge is really like. When the curtains are pulled back and the realities of policing are revealed, it's not unusual for recruits to experience a sense of awe. Not the kind associated with wonder or admiration, but more like "*awe, you mean we can't do this, but people can get away with that*?" Not surprisingly, this response is most common from those raised to respect both the uniform and the ability of the judicial system to adequately punish criminals.

So what makes the biggest impact on someone during their first days at the academy? Strangely enough, it's often something as simple as a short film clip containing just enough information to make some reconsider their career options.

"I remember my first day at the academy. We were grouped in a classroom to watch an officer survival film. The movie depicted officers performing routine jobs, such as making traffic stops and approaching a suspect's house. In the next instant, someone would blow these unfortunate officers away in graphic detail. As we sat in our seats staring at the events unfolding on the screen, a sergeant came into the classroom and discussed all the negative aspects of being a cop. This included handing out a report detailing the local officers who were assaulted the previous year, categorized by those shot, stabbed, cut, bitten, hit by cars and such. As I recall, the list was rather long.

I imagine this was done in order to eliminate those who had any doubts as to what they were getting into. It worked; our class had a few empty seats the following day."

Detective Mark Fielden, Metro Nashville TN Police Dept.

Once discussed in passing during the academy, officer survival training has risen to the top in many programs. Society is far different today than it was in 1977, when an ex-peanut farmer from Georgia was president. Domestic terrorism, school and church massacres, along with crimes associated with the spread of synthetic drugs—most notably methamphetamine—has changed the way law enforcement operates. Given these challenges, the robotic mentality of "must protect...must serve" has evolved into "must protect... must serve...*must survive.*"

In other words, it's no longer safe to patrol the streets of Mayberry armed with only a smile and a wave.

Survival training is based on the "I will do whatever it takes to survive" mindset, and is drilled into the core of a recruit's consciousness from day one. A combination of physical training, mental conditioning and emotional resolve, its purpose is simple: to help keep cops alive.

On average, two officers are shot every day in the U.S., and during the last decade, approximately 164 officers have been killed in the line of duty each year.[1] Given these statistics, survival training not only makes sense, but it's also a grim reminder that in order to protect and serve, one must stay alive in the first place.

According to Dr. Aaron J. Westrick, Ph.D., a nationally recognized law enforcement officer and ballistics expert, "The foundation of knowledge that officers possess when they first start working is found in the police academy. Citizens may have a duty to retreat, police officers do not. [As such] police academies teach fighting in conjunction and contrast to subject control. This is done to rehearse and evaluate how an officer will act when engaged in a life and death struggle when all else has failed. It tells us how they will perform in combat."[2]

"Let's be honest about this. The old 'fair fight' thing doesn't apply to our work. Cops aren't supposed to fight fair. That's why we wear body armor and have all those weapons hanging from our belts. We fight to win at all costs, because our lives and the lives of others depend on us coming out ahead not just most of the time, but every time. Besides, our goal is to go home at the end of a shift, not to a hospital or morgue. We want to go home, just like every other working person.

If we have to use force to ensure our safety, we're going to do so. That's why we won't hesitate to come down on somebody like a ton of bricks in a tornado if we need to."

Anonymous

Confronting violence is a part of the job that rookies must quickly get accustomed to. It has little in common with the choreographed fights seen on television where someone is tossed around like a bath towel and beaten into submission, but only a trickle of blood oozes from their nostrils. Real violence is usually quick, brutal and extremely bloody, and a cop has to be able to respond in kind. It's not enjoyable to watch, and it never looks good on the news when an officer is shown escalating to a high level of force. But, then again, it's not often camera footage captures the complete sequence of events leading up to a cop resorting to crippling or deadly force—the situations where they're fighting for their lives against a violent, drugged-out subject who doesn't feel any pain, or someone who feels they have nothing to lose by killing an officer before they go to prison for the rest of their lives.

"Nobody in law enforcement wants a rogue officer on the street. They make us all look bad and make our jobs that much harder when contacting the public. But in the vast majority of cases, the officers are treated the same way sexual assault victims get treated on the stand; somehow we have become the bad guys and the suspect has become the victim. It seems as though many people want us to arrest bad guys, most of whom would rather not be arrested, and not use force when the arrest goes south, even on the most violent of offenders. They can't have it both ways. If they want to live in a society where the police don't use force to arrest bad guys who are violently resisting, then they can be the ones who deal with those same individuals the next time they kick down their door in the middle of the night to rape their wives or burglarize their house to support their drug habit.

Sometimes we have to use force to arrest violent suspects. It isn't a pretty sight. Fights never are a pretty sight. Most of us have long careers ahead of us; the more fights we get in, the better chance we have of being medically retired with some sort of handicap because of that fight. We don't go out seeking fights, and in almost all cases the bad guys are the ones who get to determine what level of force we use."

Sgt. Craig Meidl, Spokane WA Police Dept.

"Some arrests require a great deal of force by us. They're just some people who'd rather die than go to jail. Resistance to being arrested isn't uncommon at all. It's something you have to anticipate every time you get ready to hook someone up. You know, some people just like to fight with the police; it may be a status thing or something to tell their friends about. These people put us in a situation where we have to protect ourselves and those around us, and they're the ones that dictate how much force we wind up using.

We're at a distinct disadvantage when we try to arrest someone. We don't know what's going on in their mind or what they're planning to do, or what kinds of alcohol or drugs they may be on, or their mental state for that matter. We just try to be prepared to do whatever it takes to get control of the subject. We have to anticipate that anyone, given the chance, will turn violent in a heartbeat."

Anonymous

Despite what Hollywood may lead some to believe, cops are taught to maintain a reactionary distance between themselves and others, so you won't often find a situation where an officer grabs someone by their shirt and pulls them close for a face-to-face "come to the alter and see the light" discussion. Realistically, it's too risky—the subject could easily ram a knee in their groin or head-butt their way out of the conversation. What makes good drama on the screen usually doesn't translate well into real encounters on the streets.

While fighting skills form the foundation of survival training, the observance of human nature is the structure built upon it. It's one reason cops stare at those they're talking to; they're not only looking for subtle signs of lying, but they're also scanning for clues that usually precede violent behavior. During situations likely to turn into a physical confrontation, officers are already mentally preparing themselves, running various scenarios through their mind while they're talking to a subject. They'll consider which way an individual will likely run, or if they choose to fight, which arm they'll use to throw a punch, based on specific signs that frequently reveal whether a person is left or right-handed.

Clues indicating violence may be imminent are often a sudden shift in body posture, the "thousand-yard stare," heightened breathing with rapid clenching and unclenching of jaw muscles, or the most telling of intentions, eyes darting towards the officer's firearm. As behavioral expert Gavin De Becker explains in his book, *The Gift of Fear*, "Perhaps the greatest experts at day-to-day high-stake predictions are police officers. Those with experience on the streets have learned about violence and its warning signs."[3]

"You view people like they're going to do something, maybe rob a place or hurt somebody. You watch for signs. You just do it all day, and can pretty well tell what someone is going to do by how they act since you deal with it on a daily basis. It's just something that's there. You know it's there, can tell it's there, but can't always describe it. You just pick up on things by watching people."

Ofc. Jerry Bennett, Washington County TN Sheriff's Office

To begin understanding a cop's behavior, you have to appreciate the defensive mindset that's poured into them at the academy and later hardened on the streets. The average person moves through the day in what's called "condition white," with their mental radar running on low power. Their mind is normally preoccupied with things other than the events occurring within their immediate vicinity. Should a distant threat emerge, they're often unaware of the danger until it's directly in front of them. By the time their mind registers the threat and switches to "condition red" (fight or flight reaction), it can be too late to mount any sort of effective response.

Cops, on the other hand, are trained to operate in "condition yellow," a state of heightened situational awareness where their mental radar is constantly evaluating all the little blips that pop up around them. They quickly assess each one for potential danger and respond accordingly. Elderly lady walking towards them with her arms wrapped around a bag of groceries? Process and disregard. Gang-banger passing nearby, one arm angled behind their back and not making eye contact? Process and react.

If you want to see how this works, stuff your hands deep into your pockets and briskly walk towards two cops standing in a parking lot. More often than not, they'll notice you without breaking conversation, and will even shift their stance or casually move their weapon hand closer to their holsters. Those serious about job survival will be evaluating your movements, analyzing why your hands are out of sight and mentally preparing themselves for a potential threat. Guaranteed. (Okay, it's really *not* a good idea to try that, but you get the meaning).

"When you come out of the academy, you do everything by the book like you've been taught. You don't get inside that inner circle with people and you maintain the defensive stance you've been taught. You don't think about it because you've done it for so many weeks, so you just hit the streets and start doing it. Then one day you think, *I bet I look like a moron in this front yard taking a karate stance when it's just grandma sitting there with her frying pan...*"
                    Sgt. Shawn Franks, Jonesborough TN Police Dept.

Hands. Cops are enamored with hands. In fact, they like them so much, they always want to see them. They don't like hands to be hidden in pockets, behind backs, underneath sweatshirts or angled away from view for any reason. Guns and knives are only lethal when a hand is attached to them, so officers tend to become very demanding when someone is reluctant to show off all ten of their digits.

Since pulling a swift judo move and tossing someone across the block isn't realistic for the average person in uniform, cops rely on numerous defensive tactics in addition to hand-to-hand combat to remain upright throughout their shift. For instance, when a stranger approaches, they may put their cruiser in gear while keeping one foot on the brake, in case of attack. It's "accidentally" sweeping a flashlight beam across someone's eyes at night and temporarily reducing their vision, thereby gaining a few extra seconds to determine if they pose any threat. It's positioning themselves at tactical angles when standing in doorways or approaching a vehicle in case someone jumps out or discharges a firearm. It's even something as simple as where they sit when grabbing a bite to eat.

"One of the most shocking things to me when I first started was something my partner said when we went to a restaurant and sat down at the table. He said, 'Do you mind if I sit so my back isn't to the door?'

And that to me was like, 'Oh my God, that—you gotta—*wow.*' So for safety reasons, now I always sit so my back is against the wall and I can see who's coming in the door. I was just shocked at the time that was how we had to think."

Ofc. Jim Long, Minneapolis MN Police Dept.

Because of their survival training, a cop's behavior can be misinterpreted more often than the prophecies in Revelations. Having a congenial personality during non-emergency calls isn't unreasonable for officers to maintain or the public to expect. Advice calls, assisting a motorist and such usually don't represent a threat, so it's easy to loosen up a little. But when a cop is facing a suspicious or volatile situation, their demeanor changes for good reason—they can't afford to let their guard down or make mistakes when anyone's safety is an issue, including theirs. Their game face goes on and it's all business.

This is especially true when officers are involved in any of the four "lethal confrontation" situations: attempting arrests, responding to a domestic disturbance, performing a traffic stop or working a robbery in progress. According to the *Street Survival Newsline* from Calibre Press, more than 70% of officer fatalities occur during one of these events.[4]

Regardless of the circumstances, when a cop switches from the "serve" to "protect" mode and exerts authority in even the most justifiable situations, not everyone is always going to be happy. And what do unhappy people do? They file complaints.

"When we go on an emergency or priority call, the first thing we have to do is quickly establish safety for ourselves and everyone else while taking control of the situation. When people are screaming, fighting or whatever, this isn't easy. Sometimes it's a juggling act—you're trying to control the scene, watching what everyone is doing around you, taking statements, telling people what to do and not to do, all the while splitting your attention to what's being called out over the radio. While doing this, we still have to look out for the unexpected. The moment you let your guard down, all bets are off.

Some people complain that we're rude, our behavior isn't what it should be, and that we issue commands instead of asking nicely. Look, when things go bad, we're not ambassadors of good will or public relations people for the city. We're cops. We enforce the law and try to bring order to chaos. That's what we do. We're not intentionally rude, it's just hard to get all touchy-feely with people when you're working under a stressful situation and trying to sort out what's going on, keep everybody safe and do what has to be done in a short amount of time. We have to handle the problem as quickly as possible then move to the next call, because someone else is waiting for help.

When we're straightening out a mess that people couldn't handle on their own—that's why they called us in the first place, you know—manners aren't our top priority."

Anonymous

If that explanation isn't convincing enough, consider this: according to FBI research, those with a laid-back "Officer Friendly" personality are more likely to be killed on duty than a defensive-minded cop.[5] While being an easygoing, tolerant individual who's hesitant to use force may be good attributes in some jobs, these personality traits are ones that, when dominant, can increase the likelihood of personal injury or death in law enforcement. Nothing drives this point home like attending the funeral of a fellow officer who let their guard down at the wrong moment.

While their cautious nature helps keeps them alive, it's their curious instincts that makes cops effective. Always evaluating the situations around them, they pick up on the little things casual observers might miss. It's like the "what doesn't fit in this picture" game kids play, but with serious consequences. *Why is that guy walking into a convenience store with a coat on in the middle of summer? Why is there a clean license plate on a car that's covered in mud? Why are there several days of newspapers on the front porch of a house that has a window open?* A mindset that's always questioning, combined with the mental discipline to constantly look for people and things seemingly out of place aren't just good patrol tactics taught at the academy. They're habits that increase the odds of returning home each evening.

Although the academy lays the groundwork of law enforcement knowledge, the consensus is the best training comes from patrol experience, for there's a huge difference between acquiring knowledge in a classroom setting and actually implementing certain skills during situations encountered on patrol. Instructors can attempt to teach everything in the book and run simulations on every scenario imaginable, but there's no substitute for experience when you're confronting a real husband and wife trying to rip the flesh off one another, or facing someone who's sticking a pistol to their head while babbling broken sentences you can't understand.

An often-cited example of the gap between what's taught in training and what actually works on the streets is the first time a rookie tries to handcuff a *"I'm not going to jail and you can't make me"* person. Despite all the impressive-looking techniques practiced at the academy, it doesn't take long to discover that sometimes the best way to cuff a combative subject is any way possible, as fast as practical. In class, the person playing the role of arrestee won't spit, kick or paw like a cornered grizzly when the cuffs come out. On the street, not everyone is going to gladly cooperate when having metal restraints locked around their wrists.

One look at how a cop is dressed will tell you they're not wearing the best outfit for a prolonged wrestling match when arresting someone. Restrictive body armor combined with all the gear on their duty belt hinders their mobility. So, the objective is to hook someone up quick, whether it's by using Plan A (a smooth cuffing technique) or Plan B (the "grip and rip" method—brute force).

Since Plan B can lead to injury, lengthy report writing, departmental scrutiny and litigation, Plan A is overwhelmingly favored by officers. Even so, the choice is not theirs to make. It all boils down to whatever option is preferred by the individual being arrested.

It's the ultimate gesture of hospitality—the arrestee gets to decide.

"It's not easy to put a pair of handcuffs on someone. People think because you get special training, you can take a person down to the ground and slap the cuffs on them like on television. It doesn't work that way. In the academy, you learn how to cuff with somebody who will go along with the plan. You get a guy out on the street, whether he's 300 pounds or 120 pounds, and if he doesn't want you to put handcuffs on him, you're not going to be able to without wrestling. A lot of times you may get the first cuff on, but once it snaps shut, the fight is on. Unless you can get someone into a real good compliant hold where they can't get away, hooking someone up can be a real challenge when they don't want to cooperate."

Sgt. Eddie Graybeal, Washington County TN Sheriff's Office

When a new officer emerges from the protective nest of the academy, they're primed to jump into the real world and flex their newfound skills in order to save mankind. Gone is the safe haven of the classroom where they had the luxury of role-playing and discussing various scenarios. Split-second decisions based on snippets of information will now have to be made under extremely stressful conditions—decisions that will not only affect people's lives, but ones that could get a cop suspended, sued or injured.

And when they wind up fighting for their lives against someone whose neck is as thick as a truck tire, the risk is high any one of the three could happen.

"Here are some of the things, as a police officer, I did or didn't think about when confronted with a 300-plus pound suspect:

I did wonder if this individual was armed. I couldn't know because he wanted to fight before I could check.

I didn't consider race. Anyone trying to stomp on me is a threat.

I did understand that no matter what kind of physical condition this man was in, I could not let him get me down on the ground and get on top of me. The sheer weight of this attacker makes it irrelevant as to whether his bulk is muscle or fat.

I did realize that if this individual got me down, he might get my gun and injure not only me, but innocent bystanders.

I did decide not to fight fair, but would fight to win. Taking someone down with a baton isn't a pretty sight, regardless of how you do it, but the citizens of Denver don't pay me to lose fights. If I need a taser, a baton, a flashlight, six more officers, a chair, a brick, or finally a gun, I will honor my oath, preserve lives, and not run away.

I did realize if I got this individual on the ground, I must get him handcuffed before he can get back on his feet. So, with that in mind, I would hit him while he is on the ground if he doesn't comply with my orders.

A Denver Police Academy exercise taught me just how hard it is to handcuff someone who will not hold his wrists still. I will use whatever force I need until he does comply and is no longer a threat.

I did remember that every call I go on, someone has a gun—me. My gun will kill me or anyone else the same as if the assailant had brought his own weapon.

I did wonder if this attacker had friends nearby that would also attack me. I had no way of knowing who was waiting and watching.

I know that most people wouldn't help me if I was losing. From experience, I can tell you that the majority of people will not jump into a fight and help a police officer. They either believe that we are being paid to handle this kind of job, or they are afraid.

I didn't think about the 'why' of what was taking place. There was never time. I had to get control and the 'whys' would come later."

Lt. James Ponzi, Denver CO Police Dept.

As they get some time under their belts, one of the biggest threats awaiting officers won't be a thug looming in the shadows brandishing a weapon. It won't be the risk of getting knocked senseless by a passing car during a traffic stop or being contaminated by the toxic residue of a smoldering meth lab. Instead, it's a threat they cannot physically prepare for—the demoralizing effects of cynicism. The *"I don't care anymore, nothing I do will really make a difference"* mindset.

Born from the despair and hopelessness of the victims they encounter, fueled by a constant barrage of dysfunctional people living dysfunctional lives, and compounded by a judicial system that is as likely to plea-bargain or dismiss cases as to convict, cynicism is the ultimate enemy. All consuming, it has the cunning ability to infect even the toughest soul, and can devour idealism and motivation over time.

This isn't to say there's any lack of fulfillment in law enforcement, for there's many positive events that help balance the scales. After all, if police work was as enjoyable as watching dung beetles consume their favorite meal, a cop's tenure would be measured in days instead of years. For those who can keep a realistic perspective on what the job entails, policing can be a rewarding and personally satisfying career. From making an arrest that puts a career criminal back in jail to simply improving a situation in someone's life, there are numerous gratifying moments on the job. And each one, no matter how short-lived or infrequent they may be, makes a cop stand a little taller, a little prouder. But often it's the disturbing events they encounter which changes their behavior over time.

Like dealing with the terror of a six-year-old who was sodomized by her alcoholic stepfather.

Having an innocent motorist die in their arms after being hit head-on by an intoxicated driver.

Entering a filthy, disease-ridden trailer where malnourished kids run around in diapers soiled with excrement, while their parents spend what few dollars they have on lottery tickets, beer and cigarettes.

And going above and beyond the call of duty, but finding their kindness was taken advantage of, or their assistance was welcomed like a nose pimple on prom night.

"I was called to a store where a 55-year-old guy was shoplifting chicken. I asked him, 'What's up, why are you shoplifting?' He was in tears, and said his family didn't have any food. For some reason, I decide to buy about $20 of food for him and his family.

The store dropped the charges since they got their stuff back, and I take him home to his family. I wish I'd never done this, but I went over and opened up their refrigerator and freezer, and guess what? A ton of food. I looked at the guy, shook my head and walked out. He never thanked me, but I didn't expect to be thanked."

Sgt. John Holthusen, Minneapolis MN Police Dept.

"My partner and I were assisting a city unit with a lock-jock request. The city officer had a female in the back of his car, but it was dark and I couldn't make out her features. She'd been wandering the parking lot of a night club, obviously intoxicated, trying to get into a Ford Explorer to retrieve her cell phone and call a friend for a ride.

She explained to the city officer that she'd lost her keys, so he called us to pop open the door for her. He was going to let her call a ride instead of arresting her for public intoxication. When my partner pops the lock on the Explorer, the female emerges from the cruiser and says, 'That's not my car after all.' Now, she couldn't remember what kind of vehicle she drove or where it was parked.

I turned when I heard her voice and immediately recognized her. She was a clerk at a local convenience store who I'd known for years. Nicest person you'd meet—would even come outside and pet my dogs when I drove up in my pickup. My wife and I even gave her a Christmas present last year.

Madder than a wet hornet, the city officer whips out the cuffs and places her under arrest. I felt bad for her, so while she's crying in the back of his patrol car, I convinced him to let me take custody of her and called for a cab. Paid the driver $40 out of my own pocket to take her home. I knew she'd feel bad about everything when she straightened out, and I'd get the money back with an apology for putting me in such an awkward situation.

Never happened. When I finally saw her again, she never offered an explanation, apology or to pay me back. Acted like nothing had happened. I soon quit going by where she worked; it was just too awkward.

When you get burned by someone you go out on a limb for, other people down the road may suffer. You think twice before making that kind of decision again."

Anonymous

Those who initially hit the streets with high ambitions and a crusader mentality seem to be the most vulnerable to developing a cynical attitude as time wears on. Within a few years of leaving the academy, these officers' perceptions of the job—even society itself—may be forever altered. Some will discover that to survive in police work, they must erect a wall around themselves to blunt the emotionally-draining aspects of the job. But as they insulate their souls from the ravages of humanity, they also risk losing the passion that brought them into law enforcement.

And that's a high price to ask anyone to pay in order to protect and serve others.

As veterans frequently caution the newest rookies, "If you're looking to change the world, be careful. It might wind up changing you instead."

*

When I first started with the department, we had the Water Street Beat, which was where one officer would go down and walk this certain area. It was always the new officer. And for the most part, guys didn't like that. But I loved it. I kept volunteering for duty. In fact, I volunteered so much they finally told me I couldn't go down there anymore.

Water Street was an area where at the beginning of the night it was no big deal. But as the middle of the evening and the end of the night approached, one officer versus 3,000 drunks is what you've got to deal with. And if I come in there with a "just the facts" attitude, the *boom, boom, boom* kind of black and white issue, I'm going to get my nose popped.

So you learn discretion, you learn more creative ways to deal with things. You solve things differently—not necessarily so legalistic. Sometimes you'd see an officer go down there and say, "By God, it's my street, my beat, and you're going to do what I say and no violations are going to be tolerated out here." They ticket everything and they arrest everybody. Other officers who had the same outlook as I would sit in our squad cars and say, "Well, in about 20 minutes we're going to be picking John up off the ground. John will be all right if he gets his nose popped once."

You know, you just wait until you get your nose popped and that will change your ideas about how you do things.

Ofc. Jack Corey, Eau Claire WI Police Dept.

*

I've trained a lot of rookie cops, and I always tell them whether you like it or not, you'll wind up going through many changes. I think in the beginning—especially if they have no prior experience—most are very naïve and sometimes immature, or at least not at the mature level you have to be at to survive on the street. And they have a lot of idealistic thoughts. They think they're going to save the world or be a hero. Sometimes this happens, but the majority of time it's not true. Mostly, you just try to keep things together. Many times you're just putting a bandage on a problem.

Sgt. John Holthusen, Minneapolis MN Police Dept.

*

I think a lot of cops go through a negative stage in the way they see the world, usually about the five or ten year stage. There's been a fair amount of research done on that, where it shows that's when cops become more cynical.

The biggest difference between officers who get cynical or burnt out and those who continue on and make it past that period is this: The ones that make it through the cynical stage are the ones that stay connected to something besides the police department. They're able to keep this job a career instead of an identity.

Calls can become stressful when you cross the line from professional to personal. A lot of cops personalize what they do too much. For too many the job becomes an identity instead of a career. I think everybody goes through this stage a little bit, but most people move out of it.

Dennis Conroy, Ph.D., police counselor
and retired officer, St. Paul MN

*

When I first got into law enforcement, it was because I wanted to help people. In the beginning, I thought it was possible to help everybody. Then you go on a domestic, do whatever you need to do to put somebody in jail, and you think it's going to help that family work things out. And then you realize—within about three months -there are just some people you can help for a single moment in time, but as far as the long term, it's just the same old thing for them. There are just some people who're going to get drunk every Friday night and fight every Friday night no matter what you do.

When you're constantly going to the same house on a domestic call and you're trying to help people with their problems, you may realize that one of the individuals could have an alcohol problem and needs to get straightened out. Well, if people don't want to be helped, then you're not going to be able to help them. That's the bottom line. You can point them in the right direction, but if they don't want to go that way, you're not going to be able to help them.

I thought going in I would be able to assist people, and by the time I retired, the city would be a better place to live. But once you become a cop, you begin to realize that after you're gone, the city isn't going to miss you a lot and it'll function without you. You'll make a difference to some, but you're not going to be able to help everybody.

I've learned not to take things personal as such. Usually it's a rookie thing. Early on you tend to take stuff way too personal, like if you lose a case in court or someone attacks you. You take it personal instead of understanding that people are fighting the law, not you. They're fighting the patch and badge. Once you learn to look at it from that perspective, it helps you function better because you're more able to let some things go.

Sgt. Scotty Carrier, Johnson City TN Police Dept.

*

When I started going to school for law enforcement, we had instructors that talked about the "asshole theory." You get into policing and the people you arrest become assholes. Then it's their buddies at the scene, they're assholes. And pretty soon, it's the crowd that's there, they're assholes. This happens over time. Then the victims you deal with, they're assholes. Then other people on your shift become assholes, and soon everybody in the department becomes assholes. It just keeps compounding because of all the negativity you see.

So, if I've changed, I guess it's in a more negative way regarding police work, because of the lack of respect for life and the complete disrespect some people have for others. People you're there to help can be very disrespectful. I really put a good effort forward trying to explain to people why we do what we do, but we still get these attitudes, "We're going to sue you; I'm going to get a lawyer," or "I'm going to call the mayor or chief." No one can reason with some people, it seems like. There are good people out there, but if you think about the ones we're going to run into, they're going to be the assholes.

Anonymous

*

When I got hired, one part of the process was being interviewed in front of a panel. They asked some real basic questions; some didn't even apply to law enforcement. Why they were asking these questions really didn't make sense to me at the time.

So at the end, they asked if I had anything else to add. I'm thinking, *of course I have something to add. I want this job.* I told them that I wanted to be a police officer because I'd like to mentor kids and be a role model and all.

There was a female on the panel who laughed at that statement. It kind of threw me for a loop, wondering what that was all about. It was disheartening, because at the time I truly meant it. So time goes on and I get trained in. The first month after training, when I'm riding around by myself, I see a little kid, no more than three-years-old. It's the middle of summer and it's hot. He was on a vacant corner lot, on the driver's side. I come around the corner and he's pushing a little dusty toy truck, so I look up at him and wave. I swear, he puts his middle finger up and follows my squad all the way around the corner—flipped me off. I drove a little further and stopped. A bunch of kids come running up to me, all excited, asking if I've got any baseball cards, football cards or whatever. So I'm talking to them, and the mother steps out on the porch and yells, "Get away from that police car! What the hell are you doing? Get away from the police!"

That really made me mad. We hear stuff like that a lot, where people don't want us talking to their kids and telling them how bad cops are.

So, has that changed me from when I first started? Well, it hasn't changed me, but it's kind of opened my eyes as far as what you're up against. It's really an uphill battle trying to reform some kids when you're going against the ingrained attitudes some older people may already have.

Sgt. Jim Novak, Minneapolis MN Police Dept.

*

New cops tend to have some idealistic thoughts about their role in law enforcement. Then they have a rude awakening.

I always tell them that old story about, you know, it seems like everybody we deal with are just the dregs of society. And it's true. But what they've got to realize is we only deal with about 5% of society; most people have little or any contact with the police. Rookies have to remember that although it seems like everybody is bad, we're dealing with only a small portion of society.

I think for awhile, you think you're going to come in and save the world and that everybody will love you. Then you get out there and somebody spits on you or tries to beat you up or kill you, and you start to wonder, *were my thoughts on life and society, were they that wrong?* It takes awhile for new cops to understand they're just running into bad people, and that there's still a lot of good people out there. We just don't deal with them as often.

That's why I encourage our officers to get out and volunteer some off-duty time doing something else, because it really reconnects you back with real society. We see stuff that will just make you sick. We see it all the time. Drunken parents with kids sitting there with nothing to eat, never getting their diapers changed, and dog crap all over the floor. And you just know that they have no chance growing up to be anything good. But I think if you get out and try to volunteer, it gives you a little better perspective on what people are really like.

Lt. Karl Fisher, Eau Claire WI Police Dept.

*

I think there's a certain amount of thought that you want to change the world, to make it a better place. Big city cops are probably a little different than smaller town cops, but it's all the same. Big city cops don't want to admit they came on idealistically, that they wanted to change everything. The reason they don't want to admit it is they come to the realization within days, weeks or months, that it doesn't really take place. You're not welcome and you're not looked upon with thankfulness for showing up. It's not like the movies where you show up and people go, "Officer, thank you for coming!"

The first year or so you can get very disillusioned as a cop. You begin to get personally frustrated, wondering if you're really making a difference. You may go from trying to make a difference to realizing you're not really going to make much of a difference to the "just screw it" mentality. That's when you become somewhat complacent and angry. And you think if you're not going to make a difference, then at least you can lay your own form of personal justice on these idiots you deal with.

After awhile, you then realize you can't do certain things to people because of Internal Affairs complaints and other problems. Then you just say, "Screw that, I'm not doing anything and you can't make me. Screw it, I ain't doing shit anymore. I'm going to my calls, do the bare minimum, and go home and just screw it. The city doesn't care about me and I don't care about the city."

Later on, you begin to realize there is a happy medium. Maybe you don't change as many lives as you anticipated on changing. Maybe it's not one a day or one a week. Maybe it's one every six months. But you begin to realize that you do change a couple of lives along the way.

Anonymous

*

A lot of people say, "Hey, you arrest the criminal, they're gone and then back out on the street the next day." But you know what? For that day, you improved things in that neighborhood and that block. You showed the good people living on the block that you care. Someone's doing something about it, and the drug dealers can't just stand there and sell their dope and the prostitutes can't be out there selling their bodies on the street. So, I think the thought of being able to make a difference and of being a person that stands between the good guys and the bad guys keeps you coming back to work. It's easy to forget that. It's easy to get caught up in the details and what you're doing, especially once you rise to the level that I'm at now. We're doing this for all the good people out there in the community that are just trying to live and work and raise families and have a good time. Those are our customers.

We really get used to dealing with the negative side of things. But every once in awhile, someone will say "thanks." Someone will poke their head out of the window and say, "Thanks for getting that guy off the street," or someone will write you a letter. There are appreciations like that, but a lot of it has to be internal. You pretty much have to realize that people appreciate it. You're not always going to hear it, because people are afraid a lot of times to come out and talk to the police, especially if they called 911 on their neighbor.

When someone writes a letter to the precinct and says, "Hey, thanks for clearing up the drug dealers on my block. Now I can let my kids ride their bikes or play out on the sidewalk. I don't have to worry about them getting shot." That's huge. That's what keeps motivating the cops.

Capt. Mike Martin, Minneapolis MN Police Dept.

*

At one point in my career, I'd be with my wife or friends and someone would ask me what I did for a living. I can honestly say I lied a few times about what I did, because I knew two things were going to happen—guaranteed. Once I tell them I'm a cop, they'll automatically have an opinion. Then they'll either ask me a ton of questions, try to pin me down on some opinion, or they'll talk about that one time they had a prick of a cop that gave them a ticket. I got to a point I didn't want to have to justify myself or explain myself anymore.

But when I was a young rookie, it was like "I hope they ask if I'm a cop because I'm gonna tell them I'm a cop. Damn right I'm a cop. Let me tell you about that bust I had or that guy I arrested," and all that other stuff. You'd do it all the time. You know, people don't do that with accountants.

"What do you do for a living?"

"I'm a CPA."

"Oh, wow, gee, what did you do the other day?"

It's like being infamous in a way. Now that I'm older, I don't mind people asking. I've gotten skilled in my abilities to end the conversation if I want to.

At some point, the stages a cop goes through become destructive. I've always said cops should never spend more than six, seven or eight years on the street, and then get the hell off. Get promoted or try something different. At that point I'm not sure if you're safe anymore because of your attitude. I used to drive around in the squad car and had a coffee cup that I'd set on the dash. On the coffee cup, it said, "Call someone who cares." And it was in my squad car facing out the window, because I didn't give a shit at that point. I tell that to people who've known me all my life and they say "that's not you." But it was me at the time. I'd roll up on a domestic and I'd be like, "I don't want to hear it anymore. You guys are like a bunch of kids. Grow up. I'm tired of this."

Once that happens, you've got to get off the street because you're not safe anymore.

Anonymous

*

Being a cop kinda goes in stages throughout your life. When you're new, you're young and everything is new and cool and you've still got a lot of adrenaline in you. It's like you're at a stage where you want everyone to know that you're a cop. You want your friends to know and you want the public to know. It's kind of cool to tell people you're a cop.

But as you get older, it's different. Now, when I have repair people come to my house, I make certain there are no uniforms hanging in the laundry room. I don't want people to know. I get sick of talking about it; everybody wants to hear a story or complain about their last traffic ticket. I've had people come up and just launch into me like, "It's bullcrap, man. I can't have a small amount of marijuana on me; it's less addictive than beer and it doesn't mess you up as much."

I'll tell them it has nothing to do with the police. Call your congressman or state legislator and get them to change the law. It's all about that attitude the police are the justice system. We're not.

Sgt. Sean McKenna, Minneapolis MN Police Dept.

*

I spent five years on the street and went from this person who had a loving wife and lots of friends outside of the job, to quite frankly, a prick. I lived and breathed this job for four years. I loved it. I'd work as much as I could. I went from the idealistic approach of making a big difference, to realizing it's very difficult to make a big difference because you're just one piece. I mean, you can help individual people on a daily basis, but to really make a change, to make people's lives better is nearly impossible because of the environment they live in. And a lot of people don't want their lives to change.

So you start thinking about that stuff when you're dealing with the worst of the worst every day. People don't realize that, you know. Cops usually aren't dealing with good people. The decent ones we do encounter, they're victims that are upset, distraught or angry. We're not dealing with people who are glad to see us or people that are happy we're there. And, of course, the crooks you're dealing with on a daily basis—the worst of the worst—they definitely don't want to see you.

So when you look at that, there's a lot of stress, and I think that changes people over time. You get very cynical—incredibly cynical—and you get this attitude that it just becomes survival. When I was out there as a street cop—and any street cop that's out there today—a lot of people say they're not very personable. The reason why is they're protective of themselves. They put up a shield around themselves and say, "I don't know what kind of situation I'm getting into next. I don't have a clue. I'm working out on the street dealing with one call after another and the next call could be very dangerous." I've told people I've been so scared I've shook from head to toe.

So when you start dealing with all that stuff—going back to my first five years—I started losing friends. My wife wasn't really happy with me and I wasn't happy with myself. I started noticing when I called my friends to get together, they didn't want to because I'd be bitching about the job or acting all big and tough. I wasn't the same friend they knew. I remember coming home one day and my wife said, "I don't think I like you anymore." That's when I decided I wasn't going to lose my wife and family for this job.

Probably one of the best moves I made in my career was going into the crime prevention unit. It made me human again. I'm still cynical, but it took the chip off my shoulder. In crime prevention, you're still dealing with some of the shitheads out there, but you're also dealing with a lot of good people who are trying to improve their lives. They're saying "enough is enough" and they want to change the standard on their block, building or neighborhood. They want to live a better life. They don't want to have crooks living on their block or have a crack house on the corner. They want to work with you, as the police department, because you're in a specialized unit and now have the time to work with them since you're not tied to a radio. They come to you and want to work with you. They're not victims yet. They're happy people and they're glad to see you. It's kind of a neat change.

Some cops say it's soft, that it's not real police work. But the last time I checked, real police work is trying to fix a problem, whether you're doing it in this fashion or any other fashion. In fact, I can honestly say that in crime prevention, I've probably fixed a hell of a lot more problems permanently than I ever did on the street. This isn't picking on the guys on the street. They just don't have the time to fix things permanently. They're too busy going from call to call to call.

Anonymous

*

A lot of times when I'm getting yelled at, I'll come back with, "Hold on, I may be wearing this uniform, but I'm human too. Take it down a notch."

I look at it as I treat people the way I would want to be treated, whether I'm a cop or in civilian clothes. But you cross that line and start treating me horribly, or you decide you want to take it up a notch, believe me, I'm going to be right there with you. I'm not going to tolerate that. I'm not disrespecting you and you don't disrespect me. That's the way I look at it.

They're a lot of us that have the same attitude. We chose this job. This was a choice we made and we understand that. It doesn't give you any rights to act or be a certain way. We chose this job, and yeah, it's not always the most pleasant, but there's a reason every single one of us is out here, a reason we've chosen this line of work. And that's because we like the job.

I can see how your view of the world can become warped, because we see all the bad stuff. But this is an amazing job and you have a real sense of responsibility. I do the best of my ability and I want to make sure in doing things right, that I'm also protecting the public. It can be a very tough balance.

Ofc. Jen Foster, Brooklyn Park MN Police Dept.

*

It's a different world out here. I wish a lot of people could step to this side of the fence and see it. Something happened to me the other day, something that's only happened once in my 13 years of law enforcement. I was sitting down eating lunch and when I got up to leave, the waitress came over and put a little piece of notebook paper on the table. I unfolded it and read it, and it was a letter from a lady who was eating lunch there with her son. It said they appreciated what law enforcement officers do, and they recognized all we do in this day and time, putting our lives on the line and such. It was a real nice letter. They just wanted to say thanks for all we do and that lunch was on them. I went to their table and sat down and spent a few minutes talking to them. They were just super nice people.

As long as I can go home and feel good about what I do—it can be something as simple as going up to a house and turning off someone's water hose that they left running accidentally—as long as you made someone's night or day, it's all worth it.

Sgt. Shawn Franks, Jonesborough TN Police Dept.

*

Why do you want to become a police officer?

"Because I want to help people," was how I answered when I processed for the police department. As corny as it sounded, I was honest with my answer. It was obviously the right answer, because I was admitted entrance into the police ranks. I imagine if I had answered in any other manner, like "Because I want to kick butt," it can be safe to say that my profession today may very well involve a spatula rather than a gun.

So I raised my right hand, swore a solemn oath and was presented with a shiny metal badge, which felt somewhat heavy. I was given bullets for my empty gun, which hangs on my belt like fate itself. Little do I know the gun will be a constant reminder of an uncertain lethal responsibility and also of my worst fear.

I look at myself in the mirror and can't help but be overwhelmed with pride. I stand there with a freshly pressed new uniform; spit shining boots, a crisp colorful police patch and new unused leather gear. Boy, I look good! I want the whole world to see me, but being a brand new rookie, I have landed the graveyard shift. Still, I don't care. Heck, I represent truth, justice and the American way. Stand back people, I am on my way to clean the streets of Albuquerque.

I report to my first day at briefing and have that pathetic smile on my face. No worry in the world, just happy to be here. A naïve cop who is going to save the world. Indeed, Superman with a pension.

But as fast as I put on the uniform, reality smacks me in the face. I soon discover a broken down machine in a judicial system that spends most of its time arguing technicalities rather than concentrating on the concept of right and wrong. And even with this, I am still required to deal with the social problems by applying laws. Except I realize laws can't solve the complex human problems and consequently, I see people literally get away with murder while the innocent cry vainly for justice. In effect, I have been saddled with a task for which I am singularly ill-equipped.

While being a cop on the streets, I quickly get a taste of the casual human violence and the daily bone-numbing boredom. Gradually, I cease to see any glitter in police work. My work primarily concerns the bad, the dirty, and the ugly side of life. The public calls my job "keeping the peace," but I feel like humanity's garbage man. I am asked to be a peacekeeper among street gang wars, a buffer between frightened victims and ruthless criminals and a social worker for families chronically in crisis.

Often enough I will be spit at, insulted in the worst profane manner and at times my life will be threatened. I feel some comfort knowing this is not personal, just the uniform I so proudly wear. When people see me they only see the uniform, while my face remains oblique and obscure. They don't see the person inside the uniform. Cops are just numbers, interchangeable parts. I will not receive any recognition, since all the hazards and difficult work are simply expected of me. After my shift is over, the only sense of accomplishment is still being in one piece; a commodity most people take for granted.

I start to envy that man with the spatula.

From the time you put on the police uniform and step out into the streets, an erosion process begins to take place. The environment, as well as the people I police, is in fact eroding me. In the wake of senseless crime and the constant confrontation with insanity, I am thrust deeper into the dark side of the American society. I see the worst impulses of men and women driven by the blindest spectrum of brutality that human intellect can concoct. I see predators that will victimize in the worst violent manner without blinking an eye. I will soon realize that violence is a way of life for me. Police work comes to be almost exclusively reactive. Still, I can't help but be affected by my surroundings. The career of confronting vicious, conscienceless criminals starts to fray upon my nerves.

It's not humanly possible to come away from all this without being touched by it. Yet, in order to function effectively as a police officer, I must be able to control my emotions.

To be impartial in the wake of brutal violence and tragedy, I must abandon part of my humanity. I do this by developing a shield to protect me from going insane. To ignore the negative aspects of the job, cops develop an aura of adolescence that is both youthful and slightly silly. Without realizing it, I use gallows humor as a defense mechanism in stressful situations to relieve tension and to defuse horror. Audiences unprepared for such graphic conversation can find it shocking and offensive.

Yes, I adapt, but not without side effects. As I look inside myself, I see the calluses growing thick and hard over my inability to feel. I have turned cynical and suspicious. I see how tarnished my ideals have become and how hard my heart is, and finally I see disappointment in myself.

The community will ignore the complexity of my problems, for they are only concerned with the solutions of increasing crime. The public prefers its innocence, not really wanting to know the violence which I am sometimes exposed to when trying to enforce the law. So, who do I turn to for support?

Having lost nearly all my faith in my community, I turn to my fellow officers for support. Only cops understand cops. The stressful conditions of the job draw us together into a kind of brotherhood, driving me deeper into the solidarity of my professional tribe.

A strong bond of camaraderie between officers is essential for my survival. My life depends on whether my partner is willing to lay his or her life on the line for me. That's why trust and loyalty is a common virtue in police work. The circle is meant for members only and has an unwritten code of silence. I feel safe inside the tribe of blue brothers and sisters—and why not? The same people that I have sworn to protect have no interest in my well-being. I begin to feel like I'm under siege from the outside world and ultimately, I start developing the classic "Us versus Them" mentality.

In briefing, I scan the faces of cops, who are very much like myself. Their uniforms worn out by age and usage, no longer gleaming but merely practical. Alienated in a corner is a new rookie with spit shining shoes and that grin without occasion. I feel a sympathetic understanding, and an odd combination of sorrow and envy. Sorrow because he will soon lose that fresh noble idealism that prompted me to join the police ranks, and envy because stripped of my humanity, I wish I had retained some of that rookie characteristic and idealism.

It's so easy to forget why I became a cop. God knows it's not the money or glory. But the rookie knows the answer so well, for he has not yet been contaminated. The immersion into the police culture can quickly strip away a rookie's idealism.

So one day, while controversy surrounds the use of deadly force in my community, a woman confronts me with burning anger in her eyes. She doesn't know me personally; rather her prejudice lies in the blue uniform.

"Is that why you became a cop? Is that why you carry a gun, so you can kill people?" Her questions pierce right to the very core of my heart and at that moment, I prefer a bullet from an assassin.

I feel like a criminal who has committed some repulsive crime. With what little shred of pride still left in me, I feel defenseless in what might be the final blow to the integrity of my uniform.

Her attack undermines the image of my profession and becomes an occasion for dismay, soul searching, and a measure of defensiveness. I can respond in many ways, but I want to seek the answer in the rookie hiding within me.

I know that despite all the violence in our society also comes some goodness in this world. This goodness is what has kept me in the game for so long. Long after I completely disaffected myself with society, I think of all the good people I have encountered. The thought puts a smile on my face, for these people are really what make it all worth it.

A surge of pride suddenly erects my posture high and forces me to hold my stomach in. I face the woman, displaying that significant smile. I respond with a corny answer, but by God it's honest.

"No, just want to help people and unfortunately sometimes you need more than a spatula."

Frozen and confused, the woman just stands there. Satisfied, I walk away, knowing I have retained that basic principle that made me a cop.

Officer Alex Marentes, Albuquerque NM Police Dept.

3

WRESTLING WITH DOMESTIC VIOLENCE

"Domestics are the worst calls to go on due to all the unknown factors—you just can't predict what the hell you're about to get into. They're the kind of calls that can make the peach fuzz on the back of your neck stand at attention."

If your only exposure to domestic violence is watching family squabbles on Court TV or viewing the theatrics of Jerry Springer's guests as they rip a jugular vein from a relative, consider yourself fortunate. You're not one of the million cases of intimate partner violence reported annually, according to the Department of Justice.[6]

As with many historical events, there is some disagreement over when the first domestic incident occurred. Evolutionists insist it probably happened during prehistoric times, when a knuckle-dragging Neanderthal came up with the bright idea of slinging a handful of dung at their mate. Creationists, on the other hand, credit the first documented domestic dispute to a young couple named Adam and Eve (when the Creator steps in and disciplines a misbehaving couple, there's serious trouble in paradise). The Garden of Eden incident has one thing in common with our present-day domestics: when "the law" shows up, not everyone is eager to take responsibility for their behavior.

It should come as no surprise that domestic violence has been around as long as relationships. Even when Columbus was disproving the notion the world was a flat slab of rock, spousal abuse was common in Europe, and was referred to as "the loving husband's means of correcting his wife's faults." A couple of generations later, British Common Law attempted to reign in this behavior. Judicial minds of the late 1700s, apparently feeling a civilized society should impose some controls on this permissive violence, reportedly issued the first decree aimed at reducing domestic injuries. Simply put, it said a man could no longer chastise his wife with a stick.

Unless that stick was slimmer than the thickness of his thumb.

Barbaric behavior by today's standards? Of course. But remember, around that time in our own enlightened country, we were tying people to a stake and setting them on fire after a jury of their peers concluded *they be witches, ye know.*

While domestic violence occurs throughout all socio-economic levels of society, studies have shown the incidence tends to increase as household income decreases. Based on their own personal observations, many cops agree.

"Affluent women who aren't working usually won't report domestic violence as often. Many don't want to lose their social status or level of living. If they don't work, they may depend on the male for income. In the poor side of town, women don't have as much to lose, so they are more likely to report abuse."
Lt. Randy Bowers, Carter County TN Sheriff's Dept.

"We don't want to stereotype unfairly, but many of these women have little education, poor communication skills, poor problem solving skills and limited employment potential. Some cops see the quandary as 'black and white'—either she gets out or she doesn't. But it's more complicated, indeed. With these life-skills limitations, these women become emotionally and socially isolated."

Sgt. Dave Cropp, Sacramento CA Police Dept.

Other than active shooter calls, domestic complaints are considered the most dangerous to an officer. According to recent FBI statistics, almost 19,000 officers were assaulted while responding to disturbance calls from 1998-2007.[7] For a cop patrolling solo, these are stomach-churning numbers to consider when rolling up to a family conflict involving alcohol and weapons at two in the morning.

Just what is it about domestics that make them so dangerous? First of all, entering someone's residence and taking charge doesn't go over very well with most people; it has a tendency to make those already mad even madder. The responding officer is often seen as an outsider who has violated the sanctuary of one's castle; someone who's meddling in a personal family affair. Add the combustible level of emotions surrounding a domestic —especially when alcohol or drugs has fueled the flames of anger—and you've got a volatile mix which can explode as violence towards the person in uniform. And with the accessibility of weapons in many homes, a cop can be standing on the wrong end of a barrel or blade before they have a chance to defend themselves.

"We recognize through experience that if we're going to have fights and shootings, domestics are a good place for them to happen. You've got the most emotionally charged situation that you're going to have other than if there's a death or something. And, you're on their territory, which is their home. You may be bursting right into their house because if they don't answer the door and there's a fight going on, we're obligated to go in.

Domestics are usually the result of something that has taken a long time to develop. You get two people who got married and were madly in love with each other. Now things have gotten to the point where they're fighting with each other, hitting each other or something else. It might be an extra-marital affair, a money problem or somebody lost a job and can't find another. What can

I do to fix that? You can give us all the training your want, but am I really going to be able to go in there and fix that in ten minutes? Some of our younger guys, 22 or 23-years-old, are going to families who have been married for *22 or 23 years*. What's he supposed to tell them that's going to straighten out their whole life so they're suddenly going to fall back in love? It's not going to happen.

We go there initially not because they're starting to have a problem and want help. We go there because they've lost control. So we go in and at least get them back in control—maybe—but the core issues are still there. Everybody in society has to realize there's nothing I'm going to be able to do in a short period of time to fix that. Somebody else has to do that. It's too big of an issue for us to fix in one night."

Lt. Karl Fisher, Eau Claire WI Police Dept.

Because of their safety concerns and the inability to actually resolve the problems which caused the domestic in the first place, these calls are high on the list of incidents officers find troubling. When being dispatched to a loud party, traffic accident or theft, they generally know what they're going to confront, so the law enforcement response is fairly cut and dried. Not so with domestics. Other than the basic information provided by dispatchers, such as complaint history at the address and whether the domestic is reportedly verbal or physical, cops are left wondering what they'll encounter when they arrive.

As such, a number of questions run through an officer's mind while heading to these calls. Will they be faced with a cop-hating, steroid-engorged bodybuilder, so huge that he has to iron his shirts on the driveway? *(When confronting someone twice their size who's intoxicated, enraged at their spouse AND despises cops, each minute it takes the responding officer's back up to arrive is sixty seconds too long)*. What if the victim winds up turning on the officer if their partner is taken into custody? *(A scenario that must always be considered)*. Will the offender have a knife or gun? *(During an emotional outburst, people often do things with a weapon they wouldn't normally consider)*. Could the perpetrator be hiding, waiting to ambush the responding officer? *(Cops have been assaulted, even killed, before they get inside the residence)*.

"Officer Billy Bowlin was walking up to the front door of a house in response to a domestic violence call, a routine he had performed dozens of times during his career. As he stepped onto the front porch, the suspect in the complaint emerged from the bushes with a scoped rifle and shot Ofc. Bowlin in the head, killing him instantly. Billy never had a chance to try and reason with his assailant, or even defend himself.

Billy's partner that evening later described to a jury that Billy's head 'exploded like a pumpkin' the instant he was shot. The death penalty was subsequently declined by the jury, and the convicted cop-killer was sentenced to life in prison. At the trial, the murder's employer stated that he was a good employee, and they wouldn't hesitate to hire him back.

So, a person kills a police officer during a domestic call, and the company he worked for thinks he has enough good qualities to give him a job again? Just when does that begin to make sense?"

Detective Mark Fielden, Metro Nashville TN Police Dept.

"I remember the first fight I got into was on a domestic. It was early in my career, when I only weighed about 140 pounds. I was by myself, about to arrest a guy for domestic violence who was 6'4" and a good 300 pounds. The guy had been drinking a little, but hadn't given me much trouble, at least until I went to put the cuffs on him. That's when all hell broke loose.

Before I knew it, he picked me up and threw me aside. I jumped on his back and applied a head lock, but it just made him madder. He slung us both into the walls, busting them open with me taking the full impact. If you had a video camera, it would've probably looked funny, although it wasn't for me at the time. If I hadn't had my vest on, I'd probably broken several ribs and injured my back from taking the force of the walls, coffee table and lamps. I wound up choking him until he passed out—hung on for dear life until he went down. When he fell backwards towards the floor, I went down with him, breaking the coffee table all to pieces. That hurt. Those tables don't snap apart like the do on TV when somebody lands on one.

The fight didn't last but a minute, but it seemed like twenty. He tore the whole living room to pieces with me. I had bruises all over my legs, arms and everywhere else. You just can't predict

how someone is going to react when putting cuffs on them, especially when it's a domestic."
Sgt. Eddie Graybeal, Washington County TN Sheriff's Office

Aside from having someone waive their Miranda rights and freely admit guilt upon arrest, most officers don't like surprises. Cops are "control people" on the job, so they don't like being caught off-guard in any situation. It goes against their training and survival instincts and reduces the tactical advantage they strive to maintain. As such, potential surprises are viewed as unknown threats, and walking into a house during a heated domestic has the potential to be the ultimate unknown. Given this, you'll usually find at least two officers responding to domestics (if staffing permits) so both officer safety and adequate control of the situation is enhanced.

All things considered, there's no such thing as a routine domestic call. A disturbing fact, since domestic complaints are among the most common incidents law enforcement responds to. Even calls that aren't initially associated with a domestic may be linked to one in some form or fashion.

"A lot of cases that don't start out as domestic violence or domestic abuse, you go there and find out that's exactly what they are. You get sent to a place for slashed tires or a broken window and you find out a spouse, a boyfriend, girlfriend, or friend of a friend has acted out. Sometimes even parking complaints wind up being related to a domestic.

I remember a guy called up to report he got this parking ticket for calendar parking and he'd never been to that block. There's no reason why he should have gotten that ticket; we kept trying to figure out how it happened. So we tried to call him back a couple of times, but never did get him. We finally got the wife and told her we're trying to deal with him on a parking ticket. There's this ticket on such and such block, and she says, 'Oh, I know about that. I'll take care of it.'

She'd been out at that address overnight and he didn't know about it. It was kind of interesting that a stupid little parking ticket was going to cause some domestic problems. I think she paid it on the sly and told him that the dumb cops didn't know what they were doing."
Ofc. Jack Corey, Eau Claire WI Police Dept.

Given the frequency of domestic complaints, some may wonder how they personally affect the responding officers. Sociologists contend the environment people work in often influences their behavior at home, so is it reasonable to assume that someone who is constantly dealing with violent, broken-down relationships may wind up having some of these issues spillover into their own household?

It depends on who you ask.

"Domesticating the abuse is so normalized, you get used to it. It makes me appreciate my spouse and how we handle disputes. If I were to do ten percent of what the abusers do to their spouses—if I was to do that to my wife—I would be separated or divorced and probably in jail a lot faster than what they experience."

*

"I think it does effect us at home, I know it does me. I get to the point where I question my kid, or the fiancé, or even family members if I'm thinking I'm being bullshitted. You kinda go into that interrogation role, and they know it."

*

"I don't think domestics have any effect on an officer's relationships, except perhaps causing them to be overly suspicious towards their spouse's fidelity, since you deal with a lot of problems caused by someone cheating."

*

"It mostly just makes me appreciate that I'm in a non-violent relationship. There's so much domestic violence out there that I feel lucky not to be a part of it. I've definitely learned that violence doesn't solve any problems, it only makes relationships worse."

*

"Working domestic violence calls does affect how you think about things when you go home. You go out on a call and see somebody being real hateful, the spouse or kids have been smacked around or something, and it actually makes you appreciate things more at the house. I always passed it off as 'these people are dysfunctional, they're screwed up in the head' until I went through my own divorce. Then I realized those people are sometimes normal folks who just got into a bad situation like I had."

*

"Domestics involving kids are the hardest. I look at these kids—they're so innocent at a young age—and they live in a house that's just a shithole, and everyone there are criminals, dealing dope and not one of them is working. And you think to yourself, if you could just take that kid, hang onto them and put that kid in a good house, they'll grow up to be a productive member of society. But if they stay there, they're not going to get that chance. That's the hard part. Those are the days you just want to go home and hug your own kids."

In most situations, when an officer arrives at a domestic where an assault has occurred, the primary aggressor is going to be arrested. Establishing who merits this title isn't always easy, for many times they'll be greeted by two angry people jabbing an accusatory finger towards one another, each with their own version of events. Even as they acknowledge there's two sides to every story, those with experience working domestics know the truth is usually found somewhere in the middle.

If one person has injuries and the other doesn't, it's fairly simple to determine who the primary aggressor was. When both subjects are injured, it's a little trickier unless you're trained to spot some of the differences between offensive (striking injuries) and defensive injuries (obtained while trying to protect oneself).

Regardless of their wounds, there are those who refuse to cast any blame on another after a domestic assault. Once these people have physically resolved their differences, it's all hugs and handshakes.

"There were these two brothers that I'll never forget. They got into a fight and one stabbed the other. Nothing real major, but one of them got a good wound on his arm and then got stabbed in the stomach, which ticked him off. So, he got a baseball bat and came up to his brother and took a homerun swing. It knocked him out—cracked open his skull. The guy ended up coming to while we were there. They were both drunk enough that neither was feeling too much pain. The ambulance was dealing with both the brothers while we were trying to get some information, like 'What happened? Why did you stab him? Why did you hit him with the baseball bat?'

Neither one of them wanted to talk to us or give us any information because they were buddies again. They refused to do anything; it was all 'I love you, brother' at that point.

That was amazing. I picture hitting my brother in the head with a bat and how mad I'd have to be to do that. Don't think I could do it."

Sgt. Steve Wickelgren, Minneapolis MN Police Dept.

While protecting the victim is a priority, officers have to be concerned with protecting themselves as well—both physically *and* financially. Let's say a cop leaves the scene of a domestic without making an arrest and someone winds up getting hurt an hour later. Like buzzards on road kill, an attorney could feast on the cop's assets if they're found liable for injuries in a civil suit. Even if it was only a verbal dispute, an officer can be held responsible for separating the parties if there's reasonable cause to believe violence is likely to erupt later on.

Prior to the latest revisions of the domestic violence laws, if officers responded to a disturbance where someone had a bloody nose or bruised cheek, they would ask the victim if they wanted to prosecute. If the victim declined, officers had little choice but to leave if they didn't witness the assault occur. The offender could boast the next day, *"the cops came by, but didn't do nothin' at all."* In reality, the officers probably wanted to make an arrest, but were often powerless to act if the victim refused to cooperate. In these situations, all they could do was walk back to their patrol unit and hope for the best.

An explanation is called for at this point. For the vast majority of misdemeanor crimes, officers have to actually witness the offense in order to make a warrantless arrest. Unless someone has significant injuries or a weapon was used during the assault (this bumps the offense up to a felony, and officers don't necessarily have to witness a felony to make an arrest), domestic assault typically falls under the umbrella definition of simple assault, which is a misdemeanor. If officers didn't see the attack take place (people with any hint of a functioning brainstem usually aren't stupid enough to punch someone in front of a cop), they didn't have legal grounds for arrest if the victim didn't want to press charges.

Most states now have domestic violence laws making this scenario obsolete. These laws give police the power of arrest in misdemeanor domestic assault situations if they have reasonable belief violence occurred. This means it's no longer necessary for officers to personally witness the attack, and they can make an arrest whether or not the victim cooperates. By giving law enforcement this power, victims who want the offender arrested but are too intimidated to demand it can breathe a little easier. In essence, the police shoulder the burden of arrest instead of the victim, and can be the "bad guys" in the offender's mind instead of the person assaulted. These days, officers are likely to exercise their arrest powers when responding to a domestic assault, or risk facing the consequences since they have responsibility for the victim's welfare once they arrive.

Since the domestic violence laws have gotten tougher, reports of family violence have decreased, according to the National Crime Victimization Survey by the Department of Justice.[8] Repeat calls to the same residence were common back when officers simply refereed or separated the parties for the evening. Now that word has gotten out someone will likely be arrested at the scene of a domestic assault, recurring complaints have declined. The question is, do these newer laws actually reduce domestic violence, or do they just stop some people from reporting it?

"An argument could be made that we pushed it a little further underground. The general impression out there is that if it's a domestic case and the cops come, then somebody's got to get arrested, somebody has to go to jail. That's not always the case. There is some discretion in there that allows us to operate, and it's based on probable cause. A 'he said, she said' won't necessarily result in an arrest. 'He said, she said' with a little physical evidence, now you're in a different ball game.

We used to get more domestic violence calls when it was the 'put them to bed' kind of deal. That's what you wound up doing, putting them to bed every night. We had this one couple, Freddy and Arlene. Every night they'd get drunk and every night they'd beat the tar out of each other. And every night they wouldn't want to have anything to do with the police. It was always somebody else calling when Freddy and Arlene were throwing each other down the stairs. By the time we'd get the call, Freddy would be just about passed out, or Arlene, she'd be passed out. One of them would go to bed and pass out and we wouldn't have to worry anymore because there was nobody else to fight with.

So we'd get calls there all the time. Seven nights a week we were at their house. Then the domestic abuse statutes came in and all of a sudden Freddy or Arlene—they were both mean drunks—would go to jail more often than not. They didn't like going to jail. They stopped calling or they'd do their fighting someplace else. We got fewer and fewer calls.

When somebody finds out they're going to get arrested, sometimes it stops the problem. Sometimes it has the positive effect it's supposed to have. Other times it just creates more tension in the household. The 'don't you call the cops or else' kind of deal."

Ofc. Jack Corey, Eau Claire WI Police Dept.

From the large metropolitan police forces to the rural sheriff's departments, there are some common domestic issues which frustrate officers. The first is when the victim only wants an officer to make the offender "stop hitting them and behave" without hooking them up and hauling them off. It's just not that simple. Once an assault has been committed, cops can't assume a parental role by telling the offender to apologize, then make them sit in a corner until they learn to play well with others. They are legally bound to take action that will, at least temporarily, cease the violence. And in situations where an officer has every right to arrest the offender even though the victim doesn't want them to, it's not uncommon for the victim to turn on the arresting officer when the handcuffs come out.

Now, instead of one problem, the officer has two.

"My partner and I were working a loud party complaint in a pretty rough neighborhood. A couple of hillbillies were having a drunken party, and this one woman was about to be beat up by her boyfriend. We called for backup because we feared there would be a fight and we didn't want it to be two of us against thirty. When he began to physically assault her, we ran into the house to arrest him. A crowd was in the house and the lights got turned off, so we're fighting as our backup arrives. Our guy, I grabbed him and got him handcuffed. I'm dragging him out the door by the handcuffs because it's just a brawl. The other three cops are fighting the crowd, keeping them back.

All of a sudden, the girl he was beating jumps up and tries to prevent me from taking him out the door. She jumps in my way, so I have to knock her down. She was light, so all it took was a push to make her fall on her rear-end. She then got up and tried to attack me again. Finally, I just picked her up and threw her out of the way while dragging him out. I think we ended up arresting her, too. That's one of the times we actually had the victim turn on us."

Lt. Mike Sauro, Minneapolis MN Police Dept.

Another universal frustration is when victims decide not to follow through with prosecution once their court date finally arrives, despite all the time and resources allocated by law enforcement in seeking a conviction. This is usually because the offender has intimidated or otherwise convinced the victim to drop the case. After the bruises and egos have healed, it's not unusual for a couple to stand before a judge, hand in hand, and explain their "misunderstanding" won't happen again.

"This condition perpetuates law enforcement's big gripe, 'why doesn't the victim just cooperate?' Or, 'they always recant, don't they?' But what some don't see is that the victim may not have any choice if they want to survive. And if they have children, they'll no doubt fail to recognize the long term benefit of leaving the abusive relationship in favor of short term or day-to-day survival. So, of course the victim may recant. However, many of these situations are actually the times we need to go the extra mile to interview and investigate the domestic violence incident."

Sgt. Dave Cropp, Sacramento CA Police Dept.

Although it's possible for the state to proceed with prosecution without the victim's cooperation, often courts will dismiss the case if the victim requests them to do so. With so many lawsuits clogging the judicial system, it's difficult for courts to devote time to cases when victims are no longer interested in seeking justice.

The sad fact is, once someone crosses the line and physically abuses another in a relationship, the overwhelming odds are they will again at some point.

*

My sister and I had been locked in the closet for about an hour when the yelling and screaming on the other side of the door finally stopped. Dad had come home drunk again, and after tossing us in the closet, proceeded to take his rage out on my mother. We were getting used to the routine, as much as two small kids could.

The closet was down the hall from the front room. It was small and dark, and had the smell of musty old clothes mixed with mothballs. *God, I hated that closet.* We had to hunch down the whole time with our knees bent because if we tried to stand, the clothes would fall off their hangers and get all tangled under our feet. That wouldn't be good, because if dad opened the door and found the closet in a mess, then we'd catch it ourselves.

Mom and dad had been going at it with more intensity than I'd ever heard. Her screams had echoed through the house while the crashing of furniture being knocked around shook the closet door. I was familiar with these sounds, and knew mom was hurting. But like the other times, I hadn't heard her fight back or cry for help. I remembered once asking her "why?" to which she replied, "Because he's your father and I love him."

Suddenly, the door opened. A large shadow filled the doorway. After being in the dark so long, the unexpected burst of light was painful to my eyes. I squinted to make out the shape looming in front of us. It was a man, but it wasn't my dad. This person had bright buttons that seemed to cover his entire chest, and in the middle of the hat he wore was a badge shining like a large silver star.

The figure at the door reached out to me with a friendly smile and took my little fingers into his big hand. Immediately, I felt safe. Maybe, I thought, this time I wouldn't have to run as fast as I could to my room and jump into bed with my clothes on, all the while praying that dad would just leave mom alone.

Mom and dad had fought many times in the past and she always paid a heavy price during his drunken outbursts. What I didn't know at the time was our neighbors had heard the screaming and "thumps" once too many that evening and had called the police.

When the policeman put dad into the car and took him away, I was confused. I couldn't understand why I wasn't mad or why I didn't feel sorry for my dad. All I knew, all that really mattered, was this big man in blue made me feel safe.

I was just nine-years-old, and that was my first contact with the police. You could say it had a lasting impact on my life. I've been a cop now for over 30 years.

Lt. Tom Frayer, Washington County TN Sheriff's Office

*

We responded to a call of shots fired inside a house. What happened was a husband had come home drunk. His wife started yelling at him about his drinking problem and they got into a physical confrontation. When the husband pulled out a gun and threatened his wife, she grabbed it and they fell to the ground, rolling around and fighting over the weapon.

A cute little two-year-old boy walked into the kitchen to see what's going on, and the gun went off, shooting him in the right side with a .38 slug. It went in one side and exited with a big gaping hole, taking most of the child's internal organs out with it.

I arrived at the front door with another officer while another squad went around back. We went in the front door as the dad runs out the back, and he's caught by the cops out there. The mother is standing in front of us holding the two-year-old. The child is bleeding and death is hanging off to the side. She's screaming,

"My baby! My baby! My baby!" At the time, we didn't know what had been going on, but knew the kid had probably been shot.

I'm yelling, "Give me the baby! Give me the baby!" so we can try and save him. She's just screaming and hysterical and won't give me the child. I end up having to fight with her to get him. We started doing CPR—mouth-to-mouth—on the baby. He must have eaten something earlier with cinnamon sugar on it, like cereal or something. I can taste it to this day, telling this story, the cinnamon sugar that was on the child's mouth.

The ambulance arrived and I rode with the child to the hospital, and had to be there when they pronounced the baby dead. Then the mom comes to the hospital and I had to be there for her. The child's clothes then became evidence and I had to collect them.

How do you go home and sleep after something like that? What do you do? It's surreal. It's almost like you're doing what you've got to do when you're there. But when it's over and you kind of look back at it, it didn't really happen. It's like a movie and you're watching it. I don't know if that's how you distance yourself from it or dissociate your feelings.

You can't just go home and tell your wife something like that, unless your wife is a cop. Now I can go home and if something is bugging me, wake up my wife and say, "We had a bad one." Kind of tell her a little bit about what happened. At least they understand what's going on.

Capt. Mike Martin, Minneapolis MN Police Dept

*

Every cop has the kind of domestic call where they walk in and see a guy wearing a plate of spaghetti or whatever, but usually it's a bit more serious.

Old Clyde was known to beat his wife, and I don't mean just smacking her every now and then, but literally beating her to a pulp. We'd been to their house a number of times on domestics. I guess Clyde was around 60 or so, and his wife was somewhere in her 50s.

Got a call there one night when Clyde decided to use a gun instead of his fists. He'd shot at her five or six times, but was so drunk, he couldn't hold the gun steady. He missed her with every round. I arrested him, but it wasn't long before he was back at home and at it again. The next time we were called out there, Clyde had taken a fireplace poker and beat his wife unmercifully. He had gotten her on the floor and literally stomped her guts out. She was bleeding internally, as well as out of her vagina. Her injuries were bad enough to cause her to go into a coma at the hospital. When she came out of it, she was never "right in the head" afterwards.

I lost count of the number of times we got a domestic call from their house. It was always the same. We'd arrest Clyde and he'd pull some time in jail for either domestic violence or aggravated assault. He'd get out and go back home, and before long, beat her again. As far as I know, it's still going on today.

Real frustrating. You arrest him, put him away for awhile, but it doesn't make any difference in the long run. His wife would still be there when he was released, take her beating and then call us for help.

Sgt. Shawn Franks, Jonesborough TN Police Dept.

*

Calls came in about a man hitting and dragging a woman. It was occurring in the parking lots of a sin-strip club and an all night Denny's Restaurant during the early morning hours around bar closing time. I responded to the radio dispatch. Upon my arrival, people were out, excited about the action they were witnessing and pointed me to where it was taking place. Good witnesses. Good statements.

On foot, I went to the "sounds-of-the-guns," so to speak. The man was dragging a woman by the hair into a brushy area at the rear of Denny's parking lot. The man didn't comply with my orders to stop. He instead moved the woman in front of his body, using her as a hide-behind shield. Whatever direction I approached him, he would move the screaming woman between himself and me. The lady was shorter than either of us, so the man's head and neck were the only targets available to me.

There's an old technique that the highway patrolmen would use to remove people from cars when the driver would lock their grip onto a steering wheel and not let go. The controlling move just involved grabbing the resister's jaw and slowly turning or twisting it in the direction that you wanted the person's body to follow.

So, I reached over the woman's head and applied the hold onto his jaw while twisting his head at the same time. The woman broke free while the man tried to spin out and break free himself—just like he would have done from a football tackler—but actually spun more into my jaw hold, making it easy for me to tilt his body back and off balance so that I could work him into an arm lock with my right hand. My left arm stayed on his collar bone and I kept him bent backwards while I talked him down and into compliance.

Another officer arrived on the scene just as the physical conflict ended. This officer grabbed onto the woman right about the time she was going to deliver an eye attack to my face, while my attention was on her assailant. She had turned on me. It happens when you least expect it. You're saving someone from further injury and then the victim winds up trying to injure you as you take their abuser into custody.

The man turned out to be a Cleveland Browns football player. The story was that he showed up at the night club and saw another man dancing with his wife. He wasn't happy, and that's when it hit the fan. He was arrested on a couple of charges. The officer who restrained the man's wife didn't tell me about her attempt to deliver an eye attack until later at the police station, so she wasn't charged with any crime.

Lt. Jim Weiss, Brook Park OH Police Dept.

*

Three of our officers were dispatched to a residence one night where a reported fight had occurred between two males. The caller advised more trouble was brewing, and one of the guys was a very violent person.

When the officers arrived, they were met by several females. One of the ladies—we'll call her Linda—was the girlfriend of the reportedly violent guy. The other females were some friends of hers that she'd been out with that evening. They told the officers they were afraid Linda was in danger and that her boyfriend was going to hurt her if given half a chance.

When the officers talked in private with Linda, she said, "No, no, he's okay. He's not bothering me. He's not going to harm me." When they went back to discuss things with her friends, they kept insisting "He'll kill her, get her out of here. Do something."

The officers again talked with Linda, but she still denied she was in any danger. She explained to them that she and her girlfriends had been out drinking at a club, and her boyfriend was just mad because she went without him.

So, here's the dilemma: Linda insists everything is okay and she'll be fine, but her friends tell the officers otherwise. The result was the officers had to leave. They really didn't have a choice, since Linda hadn't been assaulted and refused their help.

The next day, I get a call to go to the hospital on a lady who'd been violently beaten. Now, I've worked a lot of abuse cases and have seen some pretty horrible things, but I was still shocked when I saw her lying in the hospital bed. Her head was all bloated from the beating she took. Both of her eyes were black and blue and completely swollen shut. Her arms and legs were covered with scrapes and lacerations, and a huge bruise spread almost from shoulder-to-shoulder across her chest. I remember the doc telling us her head was swollen so much it was causing blood to pool down around her chest. When she cried, her tears were blood-red from all the swelling around her eyes.

It was Linda all right, and she admitted that she'd been beaten by her boyfriend. After the three officers left the night before, the boyfriend turned on her. She ran out of the house to get away from his assault, but he caught her in the yard and dragged her back inside where he beat her repeatedly with his boot. She was hit in the face so many times that she was temporarily blinded because her eyes swelled shut. We estimated the abuse continued for at least an hour, maybe longer.

Afterwards, the boyfriend put her into bed. Although she was on her period, he asked her if she wanted to have sex. What was she going to say, after she was severely beaten and almost in shock? She was scared to death and didn't want to, but said "yes" out of fear for her life. He removed her tampon and had his way with her before going to sleep.

A few hours later he woke up and freaked out when he saw all the damage he'd done to her. He called his mother and they both rushed her to the hospital. When I arrived, I carefully recorded her statement and took pictures for evidence. Over the next several weeks, I would routinely meet with her to gather photo evidence and to record her recollection of the incident as she healed. I remember she asked me several times why I was putting everything on tape.

"Because you may change your story as time goes along," I'd tell her.

"No, Mr. Bowers, I promise you I won't," she insisted each time.

I was going to charge the boyfriend with aggravated assault and rape. Due to the length and severity of the beating, the DA felt we had a good chance to go for attempted murder. I can't remember which one we decided on, because it never went to trial. The boyfriend plea bargained for a reduced sentence, which disappointed me. I'd put a lot of work into the case and knew if I could get the photos in front of a jury, we'd put him away for a long time. As it turned out, he was sentenced to just two years. When the DA advised me of the plea, he said that Linda was already changing her story and wasn't being very cooperative in the effort to prosecute her boyfriend.

A couple of months later, I happened to be going by our dispatch office when I saw Linda. She was filling out one of the envelopes people use when leaving money for a prisoner. She'd come by to leave her boyfriend some cash. I stopped and asked her why in the world she was doing it after what he did to her. She fumbled around for some words, but never gave me an answer.

What really surprised me more than anything was the boyfriend somehow convinced her by phone or letter that everything would be okay between them and to give him some money to get by while serving his sentence. You know, that's really powerful. You almost beat someone to death, and not only do they not want to prosecute, but they wind up giving you money.

Lt. Randy Bowers, Carter County TN Sheriff's Dept.

*

Domestic violence in Albuquerque is both real and extensive. Being an Albuquerque police officer, I have witnessed the violence reduce normal families to ones of fear and outright cruelty.

Early one December morning, a police dispatch took my partner and I to a call involving some sort of domestic dispute. As I was getting ready to knock on the door, my partner motioned me to hold off. He wanted me to get closer to the door and listen in for any sounds.

As we stood outside the door, we could hear the voice of a man yelling very loud. I put my head closer to the door and heard a female cry, "No, please stop! God, no!" I could clearly hear slapping sounds, giving me reason to believe that someone was being beaten. I then heard a loud *thud* sound followed by the high pitch of a scream. The sounds were too horrid to describe.

Being a rookie, I wasn't prepared to even begin coping with what was going through my head. I looked at my partner and gave him a look of urgency, pleading that we take immediate action to intervene. The seventeen-year veteran smiled and nodded his head, giving me the signal to go ahead and knock.

After we knocked on the door, a large figure of a man greeted us while keeping the door partially open, as if keeping us from looking in. I noticed traces of a dark red substance on the man's clothing, a substance I took to be blood.

"Is everything okay?" I asked while at the same time trying to look further in to the apartment. The man was trying to catch his breath and sounded like he had just participated in some extraneous event.

"Everything is okay."

"Can we come in?"

"Listen, I told you everything is okay, now if you don't have a warrant, I suggest you go away," the man turned away and started to close the door.

My partner put his foot between the door to keep it from being closed and demanded the man step aside. He still refused and suddenly my partner moved rapidly against him. With amazing force, my partner put both his elbows against the chest of the man, pinning him against the wall. This allowed me the opportunity to enter the house.

The interior resembled a typical domestic war zone. Debris of household items could be seen scattered throughout. I searched the house for other occupants. In the bedroom I heard a faint whimpering sound coming from the closet. Inside the closet in the corner was a woman crouched in a fetal position. Although her eyes were swollen, she managed to open them wide, giving me a look of sheer terror. Her face was battered beyond recognition. I caught my breath, as I'd never seen such a brutal beating.

I fumbled for my portable radio and immediately summoned medical assistance. The woman had suffered bruises and abrasions to almost every part of her body. She had two broken ribs, a fractured right arm, and would ultimately receive more than 50 stitches to her head and face.

On the floor was a wedding portrait of a once happy couple. Just like the failed dream, the glass on the portrait was shattered.

The terrified woman grasped my arm and demanded that her safety be restored. Deprived of her human dignity, she was seeking police protection from an abusive husband. She continued her firm grip on my arm and begged for protection. She was determined that society recognize and respond to her victimization.

At one point I could hear my partner having some form of scuffle with the man in the living room, but I was transfixed by the state of the victim before me. I reassured her that at least for that moment, I would not desert her. I remained at her side until she was carried from the house on a stretcher.

In the living room, my partner was standing next to the man who was now handcuffed on the floor. My partner was looking very relaxed while smoking a cigarette and he asked if I was okay. He must have noticed the effect the experience had taken on me. I ignored him and went up to the man to ask what his wife had done to deserve such a beating.

"Hey, screw you asshole, that's my wife and it's none of your business!" the man yelled as he tried to kick me.

My partner came running and held the man by the shoulder. With uncontrollable rage boiling inside of me, I grabbed the man by the front of his shirt, almost knocking my partner over. I held him against the wall and suddenly he became fearfully quiet.

"Listen, piece of shit, when you physically batter someone weaker than you and cause them harm to the point you've done, you've broken the law and now it's my business to deal with you! Do you understand?"

His eyes got wide and looked at my partner for help. He expected him to object to my aggressive actions. My partner just stood there and did nothing.

The man then looked at me and said, "Fine. Just take me to jail, okay?"

My partner decided to take him away from my grip and placed him in the back of the police car. He then came up to me and asked again if I was okay. I assured him I was, and apologized for the way I'd acted.

"Sorry, partner. I guess I lost control. I'm just so frustrated with this whole damn situation," I said, looking to the ground with a degree of shame.

He laughed and put his hand on my shoulder. "Hey, don't take it so hard. What you did was a normal response, because you aren't willing to ignore the problem like many other people do. If the judicial system reacted more like you, maybe we could stop this ugly cycle of violence. You did your part, now let the system do theirs. Let's book the asshole and go get something to eat."

We arrested the husband, and by that we started the legal action that might give his wife the courage she needed to realistically face and correct her situation.

New Mexico has enacted laws to give some protection to victims of domestic abuse. The "Warrantless Act" allows an officer to arrest a person when probable cause exists to believe the person has committed an assault or battery on a family member. This law removes the burden of initiating the prosecution from the victim, who may risk further anger from a violent man. It also temporarily removes the abuser from the family environment, preventing further violence.

Laws and police procedure continue to change in the favor of the abused victim. Domestic violence is so ingrained in our society that it's often ignored. We must respond to the question of whether we find household mayhem offensive. If we are not seriously offended, we may not perceive it as an offense.

If we are to eradicate family violence, public awareness becomes fundamental. Society, by its ignorance or acceptance of domestic violence, has allowed the continual repetition of such problems.

Ofc. Alex Marentes, Albuquerque NM Police Dept.

*

The Department of Human Services Child Protection Unit requested an officer come with them to remove two children from their home. The case worker and I arrived at the "home," which in this instance was a broken down camper-trailer that was, at best, 15 feet long. The children were approximately four and five-years-old, and were Native American from the MicMac tribe in Northern Maine.

When we arrived at the trailer, which was parked at the edge of an automobile junk yard, the owner came outside and screamed, "What the hell do you want!" At this point, I was out of my car and all alone; the case worker wouldn't get out of her car. I told him I needed to speak with mom, who soon staggered out the door, obviously drunk. When I told her I was there to remove the children, she began screaming, "No, no, don't take them from me!"

Two other "gentlemen" then emerged and began swearing at me. I was able to calm the men down somewhat and had them talk with the mother. While they were doing that, I went inside the camper-trailer.

Once inside, the foul smell made me gag. I had to take my t-shirt and bring it over my mouth and nose. I found the children lying on a wooden bench. There were empty beer bottles everywhere, not to mention the dirty dishes, cigarette butts and rotting food, all surrounded by swarming flies. I asked the children to come with me, but they just cowered into the corner. At this point, I went back outside and motioned for the case worker to get out of her car. I could see the fear in her face, but she did emerge from the vehicle.

The mother then placed all 250 pounds of herself squarely in the doorway of the trailer. I told her that I was taking the children and she needed to move. She screamed at me in her native tongue as I grabbed hold and yanked her out of the doorway. Once outside, I pushed her further away and she landed in the bushes. I quickly ran into the trailer and grabbed the two children, who were scared and crying. Back outside, I gave the kids to the case worker and told her to get the hell out of there. She loaded the kids in her car and left.

Moments later, a car full of the mother's relatives pulled in. They piled out and everyone began speaking in their native tongue. By this time, I noticed that mom had gotten out of the bushes and was speaking with the others. All of a sudden everyone started staring in my direction, giving me the feeling things were about to go downhill. I started towards my cruiser and noticed some of the relatives were reaching into their vehicle. I ran the remaining distance, jumped in and sped away. When I looked into my rear view, I saw that the relatives were holding axes in the air and shouting in my direction.

It was something I'll never forget. Domestic problems are bad in themselves, but when children are involved, it gets even worse.

Ofc. Barry Dombroski, Caribou ME Police Dept.

4

SHOULDN'T YOU BE CATCHING REAL CRIMINALS?

"Traffic enforcement saves lives, and isn't that what we're supposed to be doing, protecting people and saving lives?"

Can do work and *have to do work*. These are the two categories that virtually all patrol activities fall under.

Motor vehicle accidents, domestic assaults and burglaries in process are examples of situations requiring immediate attention, and are inked in the "things I have to do" column. This kind of policing is responsive—an event happens and officers are dispatched to handle the problem. Most of the time, cops show up after the action has taken place, then attempt to put the pieces back together.

Can do work, such as traffic enforcement, is proactive. Traffic enforcement not only reduces crashes, but also provides numerous other benefits to society, which will be touched on later. For the most part, "work I can do" is enjoyed by officers as it doesn't involve barking dogs, runaway teens or neighbor disputes. It's the chance for cops to go on the prowl, looking for opportunities to put the brakes on an activity before it accelerates into a full-blown event.

"Since the second a police officer pinned on a badge, patrol cops have debated over *have to do work* and *can do work*. The rub comes when a patrol cop, working an assigned district, goes hunting for proactive enforcement opportunities, gets tied up in some *can do work*, and cops from other districts are pressed to cover the *have to do work* calls for service, which includes the dreaded report writing. The call response officer generally complains about having to cover two districts while the hunter goes out and has all the fun. Of course, if the constant responders were doing a little hunting themselves instead of saving themselves for 'the big one,' perhaps someone would have to cover their calls for service once in awhile.

Good cops achieve a balance of call response to crime hunting. You really have to be able to do both to be balanced, effective and to make a difference in your community."

Sergeant Aaron Davis, Albany OR Police Dept.

When a cop pulls someone over for a traffic offense, it's one of the few times they approach a citizen in a law enforcement capacity without being called upon to do so. At best, it's simply viewed by the driver as a minor annoyance. Other times—like when the pen meets the paper—it becomes an expensive aggravation in their commute. Either way, officers frequently run across those who don't really want to have any contact with the police…until the time comes they need a cop to intervene on their behalf.

Since about half of all interactions between the public and police occur as a result of traffic stops, let's separate some fact from fiction regarding traffic enforcement. The statistics cited are from the National Highway Traffic Safety Administration (NHTSA), U.S. Department of Transportation.

Public: Why are you hassling me over something minor like speeding? Shouldn't you be doing some real police work instead, like maybe preventing crime?

Police: The average person is more likely to be involved in a traffic crash than be a victim of crime. Over 40,000 people die on public roads each year, and almost 3 million are injured. This isn't a hassle. A real hassle is notifying your next of kin.

Public: So what if I'm involved in a wreck? As long as I don't hurt anyone else, it's my own problem.

Police: Your problem becomes everyone's problem. The economic costs of traffic crashes—the medical bills, loss of productivity, lawsuits and collision repair, to name a few—are *significantly* more than crime, and these costs are spread among everyone through increased rates for health and auto insurance. No insurance? Then everyone else's tax dollars subsidizes your medical treatment. Those with insurance bear the burden of the uninsured with higher costs and premiums, and they're not too happy about that.

Public: What's the big deal about following another car too close or going over the speed limit? I'm experienced enough to avoid an accident.

Police: Over 20% of all fatal crashes involve "experienced" drivers who operate a vehicle in a careless manner. Frankly, we're getting a bit tired of scooping up brain matter from the highways.

Public: I just had a couple of beers. I can hold my alcohol well enough to drive.

Police: Your driving skills begin to diminish after the first drink. Over 250,000 people are injured in alcohol-related crashes each year, and 40% of all traffic fatalities involve alcohol. It's not a statistic the alcoholic beverage industry is eager to publicize.

Public: I know how this works. It's almost the end of the month and you're trying to meet your ticket quota, right?

Police: Quota? We don't have a quota; we can write as many as we want. There is some latitude in deciding whether or not to issue a ticket, though. It's called "officer discretion," and it's why one time you may get a verbal warning, and the next time you might be handed a citation.

Public: I can't believe you're writing me a ticket! I pay your salary, you know—

Police: Yes, you do. And by enforcing the traffic laws, we're hoping to keep you alive long enough for the paychecks to continue.

For police officers, the primary purpose of traffic enforcement is to make the highways safer. Since they're the ones dealing with the consequences of high-risk road behavior, their main goal is to reduce the number of mangled bodies they have to pull from wrecked vehicles. Of course, some citizens believe it's all about raising money for a cash-strapped municipality, but that's usually the last thing on a cop's mind. In fact, many resent their tickets being depended upon to generate revenue, and some even avoid writing citations for minor violations because they know how expensive fines can disrupt a family budget.

"The simple fact of the matter is that certainty of enforcement has a very direct impact on whether or not compliance will occur, and compliance results in safer highways. That's what we're looking for. If I can ensure that the highways are going to be safer by giving a ticket, then I'm all for it. As long as safety is your real reason for doing it, I have no problems with traffic enforcement.

But we're seeing a conflict in traffic law enforcement right now, because it's sometimes viewed as a revenue generator rather than for safety issues. Other than the seatbelt ticket, the smallest ticket in our state for moving violations is $138. Of that amount, only $30 is for the violation. The other $108 is for fees and assessments from the state to pay for programs, public defenders, prosecutors, judges and jail assessments. Law enforcement gets $5 for their training. Everybody else gets the rest.

They keep saying you should be writing more tickets, writing more tickets. Well, many people in law enforcement think that $138 is a pretty hefty price to pay for rolling through a stop sign or going three miles over the speed limit.

All that does is tie up the courts, because with a $138, $158 or $212 ticket, people are saying, 'By God, I'm going to have my time in court because I can't pay that.' For a lot of people, especially elderly or young families, $138 out of the family food budget really puts a hurt on them. For the state to say that you need to write more tickets so they can keep pumping these fees in order to pay for programs, many people in law enforcement find that very offensive. We didn't sign on to be revenue generators for the state.

Now you hear a lot of officers saying, 'You want to see more tickets written, drop the fines. Drop the fines down. Give me a $75 ticket I can write to somebody.' They'll accept it and they'll pay it and you'll get the safety issues handled on the street with less of an impact on the citizens and less griping back and forth."

Anonymous

"We in law enforcement don't really have much control over the statues. People tend to blame, if there's some law out there they don't like, blame the police. Take drug laws, for instance. I mean tomorrow, if Congress felt that drugs are okay and made them all legal, then it'd be legal and we wouldn't do anything. If that's what you want, that's what you get. But people still blame the police.

I don't pass the laws, but when they get passed I have to enforce them. People get angry about traffic citations being so expensive. Every time the government wants to raise taxes, they raise ten bucks to a ticket. 'That's good because people are out there violating the law and they should have to pay,' some say, until they get a ticket driving to work. Then it's, 'What? $150 for speeding?'

Well, that's set by the state. I have no control over it. That's probably why some of the traffic citations issued are so far down. Officers get to the point of saying it's ridiculous. People are screaming about these and I don't blame them. $150 is a lot of money to the average person."

Anonymous

In addition to promoting highway safety, enforcement of traffic laws carries another benefit: it helps in the identification and apprehension of criminals. One of most recognized instances involved Timothy McVeigh (the Oklahoma City bomber), who was caught after being stopped for a minor traffic violation. Discovering someone is driving on a revoked license or has an outstanding arrest warrant isn't uncommon during traffic stops. Add in the cache of illegal drugs and weapons confiscated during these encounters, and you've not only addressed a problem driver, but you may wind up putting someone behind bars before they commit another crime.

For those who quickly dismiss the odds of that happening, consider this: the vast majority of all high-speed pursuits begin as a result of a minor traffic offense, usually because the driver has something more to fear than a mere ticket.

"We have what's called the 'stolen stare.' You shine your spotlight on a car as it goes by, just to see what their reaction is. The 'stolen stare' is when they hug the steering wheel and stare straight ahead. Sometimes you'll have situations where you pull around on a car, and they'll pull over and walk up to a house, pretending that's where they live or somewhere they're visiting by knocking on the door. Then they may walk around the house and as soon as they take the corner, they'll run."

Officer Scott Taylor, Minneapolis MN Police Dept.

Despite the best of intentions, high-speed pursuits carry tremendous risks. Forget the choreographed chases from the movies, where the characters simply dust themselves off while limping away from a crash. The reality is nearly 300 people are killed each year as a result of police pursuits, according to the NHTSA. Roughly two-thirds of these deaths occur to occupants of the vehicle being pursued, while the remaining third are to pedestrians or individuals in other vehicles not involved in the chase. On average, nearly 700 pursuits take place each day somewhere in the U.S., lasting anywhere from under a minute to over an hour.

"A law enforcement pursuit is one of the most dangerous performance skills that a police officer can do. Vehicle related incidents are currently killing police at a higher rate than felonious assaults with weapons.

Some police officers do not have the correct mentality when it comes to pursuits. Though the pursuit of criminal activity is at the very heart of what a police officer wants to do, they must be conditioned to keep emotion out of the vehicle pursuit process. The 'contempt of cop' mentality is prevalent during pursuits and often times catching the suspect supersedes basic safety premises. Having the proper mindset and making good decisions go hand in hand when engaging in a police pursuit.

The current trend in progressive departments is to have restrictive policies on pursuits (i.e. violent felonies). This is effective in reducing collisions and deaths with pursuits, but many communities and agencies are timid in letting many criminals go when they fail to stop for the police. One thing is for certain—the apprehension of a suspect in a pursuit must outweigh the danger it is creating to the public."

Capt. Travis Yates, Tulsa OK Police Dept.
Team Leader, Precision Driver Training Unit

Citing political pressure as well as the mounting legal liabilities of pursuit injuries, many agencies continue to implement restrictive pursuit policies. This has a frustrating effect on officers who find it hard to accept that some motorists will be allowed to flee if they refuse to stop. They insist it's like giving an alcoholic the keys to a liquor store—you're inviting trouble once criminals learn pursuits are curtailed.

The pursuit issue remains a hotly-contested topic between the public and law enforcement since it has no clear-cut solution. To put the problem in perspective, if a burglar ransacked your home and stole all your treasured family heirlooms—even the urn containing the cremated ashes of beloved Uncle Freddy—you'd probably want the police to chase the criminal all the way to Zimbabwe. But would you feel the same way if your 16-year-old daughter was driving home late that night on the same winding, narrow road as the high-speed chase?

"An officer's worst enemy in a code-three run or pursuit is an adrenaline overload. The speed, the sound of the siren blaring, and the desire for apprehension can cause an officer's adrenaline level to soar. Once the huge adrenaline dump occurs, things can go from bad to worse. Tunnel vision and/or target fixation can set in. Fine and complex motor skills diminish, and short term memory (the creative/reasoning part of the brain) can be severely hindered, leaving an officer with nothing more than long term memory and primal, emotional instincts to operate with.

The potential for an adrenaline overload during a pursuit is tremendous, particularly for younger, inexperienced officers. One study quoted on the Discovery Channel's *High-Speed Pursuit* program proclaimed that officers involved in extended pursuits have adrenaline levels that exceed those of soldiers engaged in combat."

Sgt. Charles E. Humes, Jr., Police Training Consultant

Adrenaline spikes can't quickly be purged from the body; they take time to dissipate. Training and experience helps to reduce this excitatory neurotransmitter from being released in massive amounts, but high levels of adrenaline can still be carried over from the pursuit to the apprehension of the suspect after a chase ends, especially if the individual being arrested physically resists attempts to be taken into custody. In a hostile situation, officers don't enjoy the prospect of facing an adrenaline-filled person any more than someone would like engaging an officer whose adrenaline levels have soared.

Viewpoints aside, it all boils down to whether the dangers of letting a subject go exceed the dangers of a pursuit. For this reason, the final decision is often decided by an off-scene supervisor who can take a rational, objective look at the overall situation while not being influenced by the adrenaline of the moment.

"Pursuits are generally governed by a department's General Orders. As a supervisor, you have to decide if the dangers of a pursuit are worth the risk. I base my decisions not only on the General Orders, but what I know about the officer pursuing. Some officers may not handle the stress as well as others the minute the blue lights come on and the subject does not stop. That's an immediate 'Signal 9' [disregard]. My opinion is that we get paid to catch criminals, the public expects it, and we take an oath to do so. But we have to use common sense in doing this. Some are better at this than others, but as a supervisor you had better know who 'packs the gear' because you are ultimately responsible for their actions."

Lt. Keith Sexton, Washington County TN Sheriff's Office

Fortunately, most drivers obediently pull over when lit up by a police vehicle. During these traffic stops, cops have no idea if the person they are about to encounter is an upstanding, law-abiding citizen or a serial killer with a severed head rolling around in the trunk. As such, defensive-minded officers will be on heightened alert for anything that could possibly threaten their safety.

When you see these individuals walking towards a vehicle, you'll notice them moving cautiously, their gun hand remaining near their holster. As each step brings them closer to contact, they are quickly assessing the risk level about to be confronted. If the officer senses a potential threat during the approach, they may unsnap their holster or even draw their firearm and hold it behind their back, just beyond the driver's view. If their intuition proves false, they can easily turn and re-holster their weapon in one quick motion without most people realizing it was out in the first place.

If this routine makes anyone uptight, perhaps they'll take comfort in knowing the officer isn't exactly relaxed, either. As they exhale "licenseandregistration, please" faster than a hiccup, their eyes will be darting around the passenger compartment, taking in as much information as possible. Again, it's all about dealing with the unknown aspects of traffic stops. And, if someone *really* wants to start off the encounter on a bad note, they'll make an abrupt movement, like suddenly reaching under the seat or into the glove box as the officer approaches their vehicle. Too many cops have been shot during traffic stops to take any motion for granted (*are they reaching for a weapon, or their registration?*). They know better than to let their guard down until the encounter is over and the driver is again heading down the highway.

The vehicle pulled over isn't the only potential danger occupying an officer's mind as they exit their patrol unit. The very nature of a traffic stop often puts them in a position where they have to stand just a few feet from high-speed traffic, and a number of officers have been hit by passing motorists as a result. Highway safety tests have shown a vehicle will naturally drift towards whatever object the driver's attention is focused on, and when motorists become preoccupied with watching a traffic stop, the 2,000 pounds of mass surrounding them can unintentionally become a lethal projectile. That's one reason officers get straight to the point in these situations. It's just not healthy to remain a highway target any longer than necessary.

One of the most common arrestable offenses during traffic stops is for driving under the influence. Since the introduction of video cameras into law enforcement vehicles, a smorgasbord of police-reality shows has fed viewers a steady diet of DUI footage. As such, a basic look at this unscripted drama is in order.

"Before pulling anyone over, we've got to have probable cause to initiate a stop. You can't just stop someone because you feel like it; you've got to have a reason that will stand up in court. It's all based on the Forth Amendment, which prohibits unlawful search and seizure. But when someone sees a police car following closely behind them, especially after they've had a few drinks, it's not uncommon for them to develop a case of 'black and white fever.' They get nervous, and will usually make some driving mistake that gives us probable cause for a traffic stop."

Anonymous

Contrary to what some believe, cops don't make up sobriety tests on a whim just so they can enjoy some roadside amusement. Though some of the routines might resemble a circus act to spectators, the field sobriety tests (FSTs) are actually based on sound scientific principles—those under the influence of alcohol or drugs have difficulty performing routine tasks when their attention is divided between balance, memory and speaking. As impairment increases, people lose the ability to process information while conducting two or more activities simultaneously. And when a high level of impairment is reached, seemingly easy tasks like coordinated balance and memory recollection become a lost skill.

Putting someone through the various field sobriety tests, especially when an officer lacks backup, does carry some risks, however.

"When you're trying to demonstrate how to perform a DUI field sobriety test—we're required to actually show the subject how to do them—you risk getting assaulted or into a scuffle because you're getting out of a defensive position. Let's say you're standing there on one leg with your hands down at your side, trying to demonstrate the test. What better opportunity for a person to attack you?"

Sgt. Shawn Franks, Jonesborough TN Police Dept.

From Stinking Point, Virginia (named after the foul odor of decomposing bodies that once washed up on the shoreline) to Weed, California (what kind of weed is unclear), there is an emphasis for officers to perform the same standardized tests across the board. Currently, the NHTSA recognizes three techniques for performing FSTs: Horizontal Gaze Nystagmus (involuntary pupil movement, which becomes pronounced when alcohol or certain drugs have been ingested), the Walk-and-Turn Test and the One-Legged Stand. The results of these FSTs, along with any sensory evidence (impaired speech, alcohol on the breath, blood-shot eyes/dilated pupils) and the driving behavior which provided probable cause for the traffic stop are then combined with intoximeter or blood tests to build a case for court presentation.

When discussing DUI offenses, there are two key reasons why officers will seldom cut an offender any slack. First, they can be held liable if they let an impaired driver go, and that person continues on down the road and wrecks. As any attorney will attest, there is a tremendous amount of liability associated with an officer's actions once they've determined an individual is driving under the influence. Second, they've worked too many wrecks involving injury or death—especially to innocent motorists—caused by impaired drivers, to not acknowledge the seriousness of the event.

The bottom line is that DUI deaths are so completely preventable, they should never happen in the first place.

"Look at the World Trade Center, where we lost 3,000 people. There's outrage at that loss of life, which there should be. But we lose 15,000 to 16,000 people each year through DUI, and you feel like it's a crime. Those are people who die who shouldn't die.

One reason our society doesn't treat DUI on the same level as someone walking up and shooting somebody is because it's one here and one there. It's scattered. But if we just lined up 15,000 people and gave a drunk a car and said, 'Run over all of them and kill them right now,' there'd be outrage. I look at it as it's no different than giving a drunk a loaded gun and letting them kill somebody. They'll get the death penalty out of that, or certainly life in prison if they're drunk and walk up and shoot somebody. But yet if they're drunk and get behind the wheel of a car and run over and kill someone, a couple of years in prison and they're right back out again. I don't see the justice in that.

We could get by with fewer traffic fatalities if people would quit drinking and driving and start wearing their seat belts. If we could even get the drunk drivers to wear their seat belts, it would be an improvement."

Sgt. Scotty Carrier, Johnson City TN Police Dept.

Given that many officers have had a family member, relative or friend who has been injured or killed by an impaired driver, cops get extreme satisfaction of taking these ticking time bombs off the road. Like a big game hunter who has the ever-elusive trophy shot lined up in the crosshairs, they're not likely to just let it walk away.

Because a high number of impaired drivers take to the road every day, officers take a dim view of motorists flashing their headlights at oncoming vehicles as a warning that a patrol unit is nearby observing traffic. If an impaired driver is within the flow of traffic and is mentally able to process the alert, they may turn off the highway to avoid detection and wind up crashing into someone on a secondary road. It's happened, and will continue to until people realize their headlight warnings may be contributing to the eventual injury or death to innocent people.

Although some officers feel the current DUI laws are sufficient, many have issues with how they're upheld by the judicial system. "We don't need more laws, we just need better enforcement of the ones we already have" is a common complaint from law enforcement. From a cop's perspective, it can't be more simple—they catch a criminal, and they expect the punishment to be enforced, whether it's DUI or some other illegal activity.

"One of the frustrating parts of the job is the court system. For example, this guy was arrested for shooting a two-year-old. Same guy my partner and I had arrested a few years earlier with a gun.

On this particular day, we turned around on his car and right away he pulls over and jumps out and takes off running. It had just gotten done snowing, and he hides under a camper about 30 feet away from the car he jumped out of. We followed his footprints directly to him in the fresh snow, and on top of the footprints was a .25 caliber handgun. So, he was now a felon in possession of a weapon, which would put him away for at least eight years.

We arrested him, went to court, and my partner and I gave our testimony. Right before the case is to be presented to the jury, this particular judge throws it out and says there's not enough evidence to convict him. So I'm thinking, *'Isn't this what juries are for, to decide for themselves?'*

When judges make decisions like that, it gets to be frustrating. This type of situation happens over and over. You have to go out here knowing you did your job, and if somebody else wants to drop the ball, let them drop the ball, knowing you're not the one who did it."

Ofc. Scott Taylor, Minneapolis MN Police Dept.

Due to the financial and social implications of a DUI conviction, some people will tap into their savings, hoping a well-funded defense will ultimately get the offense dismissed. For others, plea-bargaining to a reduced charge is common, especially since the legal system favors this time-saving approach. In cases where someone is found guilty, the sentence handed down is often the bare minimum. The only consolation in these situations, cops insist, is they temporarily pulled a dangerous driver off the streets, and may have saved someone's life in the process.

"When you catch them, the courts may give a DUI offender the mandatory sentence, but there are times a person will hire an attorney who'll plea bargain a DUI down to a DWI. And what does that prove to the person? 'I got out of this with a lesser offense and I'll get out of the next one, too.' A lot of people blame the judges or the courts, but it's not them. It's the system in general. I'll get rookie officers who get beat on DUI cases and take it personally. There's no reason to take it personally. If an attorney came in and they are squared away, and you've left a hole in your case, it's their job to get that defendant off. Don't take it personal. You've done your job by getting the offender off the street."

Capt. Bryan Horton, Washington County TN Sheriff's Office

It's a common misconception of the public, again fueled by television shows, that cops immerse themselves in individual cases. In reality, they consistently deal with so many prosecutable offenses, it's generally not possible to focus on any one arrest longer than necessary to get the job done. So, if they lose a court case, whether it's a DUI or some other offense, they usually won't lose any sleep over it. Their job is to simply determine probable cause for their actions, then let the court system determine guilt or innocence. And if they don't agree with the verdict, most will walk out the courtroom door with the added knowledge of what to do better next time, then turn their attention to their next task.

All in all, traffic law enforcement can be one of the most beneficial duties performed in terms of protecting property and saving lives, but it often remains a thankless endeavor. While some may extend an appreciative handshake to an officer for saving them from an assault or catching the burglar who ransacked their home, not many people want to hug a cop after being issued a citation.

"Our job is law enforcement—to enforce all statutes whether we believe in them or not. If we start enforcing only the ones we believe in—well, that's pretty much what a dictator does. Our role is to investigate all crimes, big and small. Parking tickets to murders and everything in between.

When people minimize traffic enforcement, maybe say we are wasting our time and there are more important things to do, we can show them where we have more loss of life, more injury and more loss of money from accidents than from burglaries or any other crime you can think of. Really, we can help society the most by doing more traffic enforcement and less burglary patrol."

Lt. Karl Fisher, Eau Claire WI Police Dept.

"Some people want you to cruise businesses, patrol neighborhoods and solve crimes. That does have a role in law enforcement, don't get me wrong. But a lot of times, through traffic enforcement, we prevent other problems. Traffic collisions cost billions of dollars each year to our economy. Traffic enforcement is also a tool to be used as a deterrent for people who are thinking of committing crimes, thinking of breaking into a business tonight. Lo and behold, you pull them over on a traffic stop and find fruits of the crime in their vehicle. You find things that tell you something just isn't right—these guys out at two in the morning and you pull them over with a tail light out or something of that nature.

I'm not advocating pulling over cars all night long, but it certainly does have a role in that you're able to stop people and come across things to solve crimes because of traffic enforcement. If you see a car just driving around at random at two in the morning, as a police officer that ought to raise suspicion, or at least it should be worth a look.

I know it's not illegal to drive around at night, but at two in the morning, if you have a reason to pull someone over, you may find out they're up to no good."

Sgt. Scotty Carrier, Johnson City TN Police Dept.

*

My first call was a chase. It was a Sunday night, about 1:30 in the morning. I was driving down a road towards the university, almost kind of dazing. You know, when you drive and just relax. I had the radio on, there were no calls, and the students were gone. A K-9 unit from the city called out and said he just passed a car coming down a hill—which he clocked at over 80 miles an hour—but wasn't able to turn around on it.

That kind of caught my attention. When the call came out, I was driving and minding my own business. I was half a block away from the intersection of Summit and Fairhaven when I saw the car fly past the stop sign. It was going so fast that it actually went airborne as it shot through the intersection. If I'd arrived a few seconds sooner, it would've T-boned me.

As I attempted to catch up to the car, it went into a yard and tried to make a turn. It came out on Main Street and ran another stop sign, completely disregarding traffic. When the car accelerated, I knew I was in a pursuit. I notified dispatch as I chased him up a hill around 75 miles an hour. At the top of the hill, the car suddenly veered right, slammed on the brakes and stopped. I pulled in behind them and stopped as well.

I didn't have any backup or anything, and since there were two guys in the car, I just opened my door and waited to see what they would do. Evidently, they were trying to bait me out of my cruiser. When they realized I wasn't budging, they took off. I slammed my door and the pursuit was on again. Just as I caught up with them the second time, they slowed to a stop.

The situation now turns into a felony stop—guns are drawn and people are ordered out of the car and brought back handcuffed. In a way, it was kind of fun and exciting because it was such a rush. It dawned on me afterwards how serious it was because the driver was disregarding traffic. He obviously didn't care about the innocent people on the roads. Plus, the driver and passenger were both intoxicated and high on marijuana.

Turned out the driver had outstanding felony warrants for his arrest. When he was searched, $2,500 in cash was found in his front right pocket. In the trunk were two large duffle bags full of marijuana. And the passenger, we found out, was on parole for murder.

Pointing a loaded firearm at someone you're looking at is a situation you don't really recover from right away. It sits with you a long time. You have an adrenaline rush and your thoughts are racing. It's a nervous, extreme high.

When you sit down and think about it, it's serious. A lot of liability. A lot of stuff to deal with.

Anonymous

*

I never felt stressed about the whole danger part of the job. It's all the second-guessing that I find stressful. "Oh, I have to go down an alley after a guy with a gun? Well, I have a gun too, and he'd better be more afraid of me than I am of him." That's sort of the attitude I always took.

I was in a wicked chase one time, and this was back in the time when we were a little more liberal about pursuits. A guy had pulled up in front of his friend's house and started laying down on his damn horn. Well, somebody got tired of it and called the cops. When I arrived, the guy started driving away, so I pulled him over. He gives me some state ID, so I know right away he didn't have a license. It's 10 minutes to quitting time, so I'm going to just write him a ticket and tell him to leave the car at the curb, and watch him walk away before I head out. If he gets back in after I leave, I don't care. I'd be issuing him a lawful order and if he breaks it, it's on him. Bottom line is that I would still get to go home on time.

All of a sudden, he takes off while I'm writing the ticket, so it's off to the races at four in the morning. We get out onto the highway and when we're almost to the steps of the state capitol, a state patrolman comes in from behind the guy and gives him that 'chase termination' deal. The guy's car doesn't just flip over—it does cartwheels down the highway. Tires are flying off with pieces of the car, and I'm thinking, "This guy's dead. I know he is. And I'm going to have to explain why I chased him when I was holding his ID."

The thought of that was stressful. The idea of being in a chase at over 100 miles an hour wasn't. The inevitable second-guessing is what was stressful.

Anonymous

*

Some years ago, I stopped a typical drunk driver. The car was weaving all over the roadway and only traveling at about 15 miles an hour. It was well after bar closing time and the streets were deserted. The car appeared to be occupied by only a male driver. I stopped the vehicle and made my approach.

I couldn't believe what my eyes were seeing. The man had stopped the car but was still continuing to "drive" the steering wheel. He was staring straight ahead and didn't see me standing beside the car. He was obviously highly intoxicated. Now I know that many experienced officers have observed this same behavior, but this one had a slight twist—there was a woman passed out in the driver's lap. The woman's mouth was wide open and she was unconscious from alcohol consumption. Inside her mouth was the man's exposed flaccid penis. The guy was quite well endowed.

I talked to him and received no response at first. I had to yell and shine a flashlight in his eyes to get his attention. When I ordered him out of the car, he grunted and tried to emerge from the vehicle. This resulted in the woman's head being pushed against the steering wheel and the driver being thrown back into the seat as if someone had yanked him back inside. The woman moaned. The driver looked at his lap in amazement, grunted, then picked the woman's head up and shoved her to a semi-seated position in the passenger side of the car. Still, she didn't wake up.

The driver exited the car with his manhood dangling in the breeze. I spoke with him, but conversation was difficult with his severe degree of intoxication. I was eventually able to communicate that he was exposing himself and needed to put the horse back in the corral. He hesitated, tilted his head, and then looked down towards his feet. He grunted and used what little dexterity his fingers had left to put things away.

Needless to say, the man was arrested and taken to jail. The woman was released to a friend.

Sgt. Jim Rose, Delaware OH Police Dept.

*

We were working a day shift, it was on a weekday. One of our officers got a domestic call in Fall Branch. I followed behind him down the interstate and as we got off the exit ramp, I got caught up in some traffic. All of a sudden, directly in front of me, a pickup truck runs up underneath a dump truck. Evidently, the driver wasn't paying attention to the dump truck stopping in front of him.

The bed of the dump truck crashed down on the cab of the pickup. I locked my brakes and jumped out. The driver of the dump truck did the same, and we both ran to the pickup. Inside was a male, probably in his thirties. The guy was trapped from the waist down where the dashboard had collapsed on him. He was looking right at me and screaming, "Get me out! Get me out!" I tried to pull him out of the vehicle, but the doors were buckled in around him. The next thing I know the pickup caught fire. The cab becomes engulfed, and the guy is just looking at me, screaming for me to help him. I've never seen anyone as scared as he was.

About that time I felt two hands grab me from behind and pull me away. They'd dragged me back about 15 feet when the pickup exploded. Fire completely engulfed the guy. He burned alive right in front of me, all the while screaming in pain. One minute he's alive, driving along, and the next minute he's dead. All because he didn't notice a dump truck had stopped in front of him.

I never got over that accident. I just don't think about it as much now, but I've never gotten over it.

Capt. Bryan Horton, Washington County TN Sheriff's Office

*

I responded to a wreck one night back when I was a motorcycle cop. It involved a husband and wife who'd been ejected from a vehicle and killed. Within the twisted metal was an empty infant car seat. Me and the other officers on the scene frantically searched the area for a child, but never found one. A wrecker soon arrived to tow the car. After he pulled up to attach the vehicle, the wrecker operator let out a scream. I'll never, ever forget what it sounded like.

He was standing next to his tow truck, staring down at the wheels. Embedded between the double tires in the rear was the child, crushed to the point of non-recognition.

People want to know just how and why police work can change you. How can you witness horrors like that and not be changed?
Lt. Tom Frayer, Washington County TN Sheriff's Office

*

I think a lot of cops remember their first dead body. Up to that point, you always wonder how you'll act, you know, what it'll look like and things like that.

The first corpse I saw was during a traffic accident, or traffic crash, as they're called now. Late one night a guy driving a mid-size car drifted across the dividing line on a two-lane road and hit a large pickup truck traveling in the opposite direction. When we arrived, it quickly became obvious how bad the crash was for one of the vehicles; the front of the car that caused the wreck was crushed like an aluminum can. I knew there wasn't any way the driver was going to be alive. The people in the pickup were shaken up a bit, but were okay.

I made my way over to the twisted metal of the car and looked inside the crushed interior. A white male, mid-thirties, was slumped over the wheel. A large gash ran across his head, probably where the steering wheel rammed itself into his skull. His head was turned awkwardly to the left and his face had already started turning that pasty-gray color from a lack of blood circulation. His eyes were wide open, but there was nothing for him to see anymore. The distinct odor of death—you'll always remember it once you've whiffed it—was all around the body.

The irony of the whole situation hit me when I glanced down and saw his right arm resting on the center console. Despite the violent impact, his fingers were still tightly wrapped around a can of beer, like some sort of death-grip. Precious cargo, I guess.

I remember not feeling a whole lot for the victim. The feelings instead came when I looked into his wallet for identification, and saw a picture of him with his wife and kids. That hurt, thinking of the family who has to suffer the emotional grief of losing their loved one over something as stupid as drunk driving. A young wife left without her husband, and two cute kids who wouldn't have their father around anymore. All because he got drunk and drove.

For awhile, I was ashamed that I didn't feel any sympathy for the guy. When I talked to other officers later, I learned those feelings—or lack of them—wasn't uncommon. Off the record, a lot of cops will tell you their sympathy goes out to the innocent people who are hurt in a wreck caused by an impaired driver, but it's less common for an officer to get emotional when someone drives drunk and just kills themselves. They brought it on themselves, and there's no one to blame but themselves. I know cops who literally breathe a sigh of relief when they walk up to a DUI wreck and find the impaired driver was the only one injured or killed.

I've worked a number of DUI fatalities since that night, and it's always the same. I feel bad for the innocent victims and the family of the offender, but not the offender themselves.

Anonymous

5

FIVE POUNDS OF TRIGGER PULL

*"One of the most frequent questions we hear is,
'Have you ever shot someone?' It's like being a weightlifter
and everyone asking how much you can press."*

One of the most common firearms officers carry is manufactured by Glock. On average, it takes about five pounds of pressure on the trigger (called trigger pull) to discharge a round from one of these weapons.

And when a cop takes a life, it's the heaviest five pounds they'll carry for the rest of their days.

There is a phenomenon in law enforcement known as *suicide by cop* or *police-assisted suicide*. It refers to a suicidal person who intentionally creates an imminent threat of serious harm or death to an officer or other individual, which forces the officer to respond with deadly force. In layman's terms, it's when someone willingly makes a cop kill them.

"We've had one [suicide by cop] that was successful here. Those are very confusing. They instill a lot of anger on our part. Why are they making us be a part of that? If the guy's got that much of a problem, just go do it. Don't take anybody with you. If you've got your problems and that's the best you can come up with, then settle it yourself."

Anonymous

While the suicidal person may ultimately achieve their death wish, it's the officer drawn into the ordeal who must live with the consequences of the experience. According to the Police Psychology Consultation Center in Delaware, 85% of the officers involved in these incidents suffer a serious emotional fallout afterwards.[9] A contributing factor to this trauma is most police shootings take place at a distance of less than 15 feet from the subject, many within touching distance of the individual. When you can immediately see the damage a bullet causes as it rips through flesh, taking a life becomes an up close and personal experience.

"We don't like it. We're wired to save people. We're wired to have successful outcomes. We like to think we are very practically oriented; solve the problems. Don't do something stupid. Suicide, a lot of times, is viewed as something stupid and cowardly. It's a very selfish act, not thinking of the other people affected by it. It's not just you, you know. TV has given us the big facade of being emotionless. We can handle anything; shoot a guy. But it does affect us if somebody dies in our presence if our acts don't prevent the death. We don't like them [suicide by cop]. We worry about it a lot. It will have an emotional aftereffect on you."

Officer Jack Corey, Eau Claire WI Police Dept.

Cops must have the mindset they can, and will, pull the trigger without hesitation if a situation calls for it. Their jobs, as well as the public they've taken an oath to protect, demand that discipline. Many feel pulling the trigger is the easy part; it's what they're trained to do when necessary and should be an instinctive response to a deadly threat. The hard part is dealing with the potential consequences of discharging their firearm—the departmental investigations, civil lawsuits, media scrutiny, people second-guessing their actions, and the emotional turmoil they'll struggle with long after the incident has faded from news coverage.

"You have to protect people and you've got to protect yourself. If you can't do it, get the hell out. There's just no sugarcoating it. If you can't take a life, don't do this job. If you have to second-guess yourself, you're taking too much time in these situations. Action always beats reaction, and if you're going to have to kill someone and take a second to think about it, you're probably going to be too late. When you're dealing with someone who wants to hurt you, and the little hairs are standing up on the back of your neck, you shouldn't be thinking. You should be reacting. Otherwise, you're going to get hurt.

When I came on, almost all the training was how to protect yourself and your partner, how to take someone to the ground as fast as possible without getting hurt yourself. How to fight and whatever; everything was very physical. Now, we're teaching new cops how to be nice to people. And that's not bad in itself; it's just we're not dealing with nice people. We're allowing society to dictate to us that we have to be nice to everybody. If you take these people and throw them in front of the shit heads, they're not going to be nice. They're going to be afraid.

We don't want to kill anybody. We just want to stop the threat. Sometimes the only way to do that is to pull the trigger."

Anonymous

"One time we had a guy who had a gun in his waistband. We were looking for somebody shooting a gun off in the middle of the day. A sergeant comes up and stops and yells for these two guys to put their hands on top of the car. I'm across the street and I can see the gun in the waistband, but the other cops can't because they're walking around the squad car.

So, I got my gun right on him, and I'm yelling for him not to touch his gun. He grabs his waist, grabs the gun and was pulling the damn thing—a .45—out of his waistband. Could I have shot him? Certainly. How long would it have taken him to turn that gun on me and shoot? I couldn't have reacted fast enough to him shooting. It's been proven time and time again. You can't do it. Scientifically, it's been proven.

But, I had my gun right on him, and was just waiting for his wrist to cock just a little bit. Had he turned that gun at all, I would've fired. I know I would have, but I didn't. It's all in that split second, and that split second could've turned out to be a problem for him. As it turned out, he pulled the gun out and dropped it straight down."

Sgt. Jim Novak, Minneapolis MN Police Dept.

Whenever an officer has to resort to deadly force with a firearm, there are always those who ask, "Why can't cops just shoot someone in the arm or leg? Why do they always have to try and kill someone?" At first glance, this question seems reasonable. But in reality, aiming for an appendage isn't practical for several reasons.

The odds of intentionally hitting a relatively small, moving target such as an arm or leg in a lethal confrontation are quite low. Adding to this difficulty is when an officer is in a shooting situation their adrenaline levels are spiking, which interferes with the fine motor skills needed for specific shot placement. Also, taking the time to aim for a fast-moving limb under stressful conditions wastes precious seconds...seconds that can get them killed when facing an armed attacker.

"The courts have recognized and it's been demonstrated that if somebody is within 21 feet of you and has a knife, they can stick it in you before you can shoot them. We know that is our danger zone. If you're within the 21 feet area of someone with a knife, you are in a deadly zone. We need to shoot you or you need to back off."

Anonymous Tactical Response Unit Commander

This is why street cops are trained to aim for center mass (area extending from just below the shoulders to above the waist) in order to stop the threat. It's the largest and easiest target to immediately acquire in stressful conditions, doesn't flail like arms and legs, and the likelihood of ending the confrontation is greater since the vital organs reside in this area. Ask yourself this question...if your life was in jeopardy, would you want an officer to attempt to wing the offender in the arm (and likely miss), or shoot at center mass to stop the attack?

Regardless of the circumstances, the aftermath of ending a life is difficult. No one ever signs on with the goal or intent to kill somebody, but it's a potential part of the job that must be acknowledged, and anyone sticking a badge on their chest has to be mentally prepared to take one life to save another. As street wisdom dictates, "It's better to be judged by a jury of twelve than carried by six pallbearers."

"What's hard to deal with out here is the lack of respect for life. There's countless numbers of times where I've responded to shootings, homicides, stabbings and suicides. There are a lot of cold-blooded people out there, and that bothers me. People who wouldn't think twice about shooting you for any number of reasons, you name them. They will kill and not think about it, whereas if I had a justifiable shooting out there, that would bother me."

Sgt. Jim Novak, Minneapolis MN Police Dept.

After a lethal confrontation, some officers are able to cope and continue on. They put the issue to rest, convinced they did what the situation forced them to do. Others don't fare as well. Unable to come to terms with the consequences of pulling the trigger, some choose to leave law enforcement while others fall into a deep state of depression and guilt. Unfortunately, a few within this group ultimately decide the only way to shed the emotional burden of taking a life is by ending their own.

Just how prevalent is suicide by cop? Unless there's clear and convincing evidence indicating such, suicide by cop is often classified as a justifiable homicide, which makes it difficult to put an accurate number to it. A landmark study which appeared in *Annals of Emergency Medicine* suggested that in Los Angeles County alone, 46 out of 437 officer-involved shootings during an 11-year period were provoked by people intent on committing suicide.[10] Those incidents involved males 98% of the time, and many had a history littered with previous suicide attempts, alcohol or drug abuse and domestic violence. In a number of these cases, the recent breakdown of a relationship was a common thread among the perpetrators. And, according to the authors of this study, suicide by cop appears to be on the rise.

"I think suicide by cop involves people who just want to die, not that they want to die at the hands of officers. That's just a convenient methodology. It's people who typically lack the courage to commit suicide by themselves. I've counseled way too many officers involved in these situations."

Dennis Conroy, Ph.D., police counselor
and retired officer, St. Paul MN

Many of those attempting suicide by cop fall under the umbrella definition of EDP (emotionally distressed person). According to the U.S. Surgeon General's Office, 21% of the adult population suffers from mental disorders at any given time, and 5% of these disorders are serious in nature. As our overcrowded and underfunded mental institutions are forced to release patients prematurely, the potential for cops to encounter an EDP has increased. In fact, some professionals estimate around 20% of all officer encounters involves EDPs.

"We do get a fair amount of calls dealing with mentally ill people. Many times you don't know about a person being mentally ill unless you've been there before. You can tell when they're off their medication when Satan's in the room and they can't get him out, or there's different people hiding in paper bags inside the house. You may tell them, 'Okay, let's go and talk to somebody about this,' and they say, 'Wait just a minute, God's talking to me on the radio, and as soon as He's done, we can go."

Officer Scott Taylor, Minneapolis MN Police Dept.

The likelihood for irrational behavior and unprovoked violence can be higher with these individuals, which presents a number of challenges those on street patrol are not equipped to handle. Identifying an EDP during a brief encounter can be difficult, for the signs and symptoms vary between people. However, it's safe to assume if someone who never served in the military is having flashbacks to combat battle in Vietnam, they probably have a mental disorder.

"Some people think that because a person is mentally ill, they're not dangerous. Mentally ill people, throughout my entire career, they've killed family members, killed strangers, so on and so forth. Regardless of whether or not a person is mentally ill, if they are threatening someone with deadly force, you have to respond in like. It's sad, but a lot of things the police have to do are sad. It's not taken lightly, but it's part of our job. We're the last resort after the counselors, social workers and therapists.

If you don't think you can do something like this, then you shouldn't be a police officer. I'm kind of amazed at the people who say, 'I didn't know I would've had to do that.' That's what police officers sometimes have to do, unfortunately. It's a sad phenomenon, but what are you going to do when someone has a gun pointed at you?"

Lt. Mike Sauro, Minneapolis MN Police Dept.

Dealing with an armed suicidal person is extremely dangerous, and what you see on television isn't necessarily what transpires in real life. "Some people attempt suicide by cop because they want to leave the ultimate decision up to someone else, and who better than a police officer," points out Hal Brown, a licensed clinical social worker in Massachusetts who has researched and counseled law enforcement professionals on the subject. "Television police dramas sometimes depict police officers doing exactly the wrong thing with armed suicidal people. How often have you seen the caring officer on television talk someone who is suicidal into handing over his knife or gun? It makes good drama, but in real life this is an exceedingly risky tactic because that person may turn on the officer."

Brown explains that somebody who has decided to assault an officer in order to provoke a lethal confrontation has committed a criminal act. Even threatening an officer or civilian with a weapon, whether it's loaded, unloaded or fake is a crime as well. "One thing that all these people have in common...is the person who commits suicide by cop has by definition gone from being a victim to being a perpetrator," he concludes.

When discussing the subject of using deadly force, it's important to understand that law enforcement agencies have specific guidelines governing the utilization of force. It's a principal based on escalating force to the appropriate level to meet the immediate threat. And although a step-wise approach in determining the use of force flows logically on paper, its real-world application is dependent on the threat level perceived by an officer in a matter of seconds.

"The escalation and de-escalation of force according to the officer perceptions of the subject threat action should be emphasized. The officer's duty to protect and serve must be emphasized along with consideration of the violent, stressful and dynamic situations in which the policies will truly be applied.

Officers do not have to use the 'minimum force' necessary. The law is clear that reasonable force must be used. In fact, when considering the most common method of police countermeasure (force) usage, a 'Plus One' rule is cited. This rule advocates a use of force strategy that is one continuum level above the officer perceived suspect force threat."

Aaron J. Westrick, Ph.D., Charlevoix County MI Sheriff's Dept.

The following illustrates a progressive force continuum used by some departments:

1. Officer presence (even the presence of an officer can be considered a forceful action)
2. Verbal warnings/commands
3. Chemical agent
4. Impact weapon (baton)
5. Hands-on techniques
6. Deadly force

The last option is obviously controlled by the most stringent policies. Generally, using deadly force is only considered appropriate when it's necessary to protect individuals (including the officer) from serious physical injury or potential death, and the threat of such is imminent.

It bears mentioning that officers don't always have to go step-by-step in increasing their application of force. Departmental guidelines allow room for discretion, as threatening conditions can change in a second. For example, a person's career in law enforcement would be cut short if they were required to try an arm lock before resorting to deadly force against someone threatening them with a knife, and common sense dictates that cops who want to go home at the end of a shift aren't going to grab their baton in a gunfight. As such, officers may justifiably skip several levels when selecting the appropriate amount of force to use against a specific threat.

And when that threat becomes a situation requiring five pounds of trigger pull, all officers speak with one voice. They want to save lives, not take them.

*

I can remember two instances where we were facing a potential suicide by cop situation.

On the first one, we got called to a house by a lady who said her son was acting crazy with a machete. The place was a wreck. When officers went up to the bedroom where the son was, he opened the door, machete in hand. Well, the officers drew their weapons and had everyone else get out of the house. He kept opening and shutting the door while the officers were talking to him.

I got up there and brought in one of our less-lethal guns, which I carried in our truck. We're talking to the guy and it was obvious to me that he wasn't about to give up. I called in for the rest of the tactical team, just like any supervisor does. I recommended we get a negotiator up there and call in several more people. We'd already cut off his phone lines so he didn't have access to the phone in his bedroom.

We were standing in this small part of the hallway, trying to talk to him through the door. Just like that, he opened the door and started walking towards us, machete still in hand.

"All right, time's up," he said.

I fired the first shot. I still had the gun down at my hip and didn't have time to aim at him since he was probably about only 12 feet away. It hit him in the arm and he kind of stopped. So, I shot him again—this time in the chest.

Part of the surprise of getting shot with these rounds is most people don't know what it feels like to get shot. You can imagine what it looks like. The sounds, the feel and all those things. Well, that's part of the dilemma with less-lethal weapons; people get the impression they are being shot and killed, so of course they react in a certain way by falling down and things like that. The less-lethal rounds just plain hurt. We use them like a long baton; rather than hitting somebody in the knee or elbow, you're hitting them from 12 feet away instead.

So anyway, when I hit him in the chest, he stopped and froze. Since he still had the machete, I hit him with another round. All this time we're yelling, "Drop it! Drop it!"

All of a sudden he realized that even though the rounds hurt, he wasn't being killed. He started to run to a couch. I fired four more rounds. I hit him every time—in the chest, in the side, in the back area. By the time he got to the couch, he just threw the machete.

"That's enough!" he yelled. He gave up.

The second case involved, I think, the first person we ever shot with a less-lethal round. He was a suicidal guy we'd been looking for, and we had him pinned in a dead-end street. So he's stuck there, and we're about 70 feet away from him. He kept holding a gun to his head. He was looking towards us, and behind us was a large shopping mall. It was 7:00 at night and all kinds of people had gathered even though we'd closed off the street.

The guy starts saying, "If I shoot you guys, you're going to have to kill me." Again, another suicide by cop situation. "If I walk at you and start pulling the trigger, you're going to have to shoot me, so just shoot me now," he said.

Of course, we didn't want to shoot him. If he starts walking toward us, fires a shot and kills one of the citizens behind us, people are going to say, "Why didn't you shoot him sooner?" You know, we can't win. Either we don't shoot him soon enough or we shoot him too soon. Well, we had the less-lethal and we ended up shooting him with that. We hit him in the arm and he dropped the gun and the thing was over.

If I didn't have the less-lethal in my hand, I would have fired my gun, without question. There's no doubt and nobody would have ever questioned it.

Lt. Karl Fisher, Eau Claire WI Police Dept.

*

It was Christmas Eve and we got a call of a possible suicide/shots fired. It involved an older guy, around 72, who was dying of cancer. The guy had taken his pistol, and told his wife to go to the store. He then put the gun to his head and pulled the trigger, but twitched—as it so often happens—which caused him to shoot both his eyes out as well as half his nose. He didn't die; he was still alive. One eye was over there, and the other was hanging from his face.

I remember getting there; my partner and I were the first ones to arrive. The guy was on the ground, feeling around for something. At first we couldn't figure out what he was doing. We soon discovered he'd originally loaded only one round in the gun and wanted another one to finish the job. When he shot himself, he knocked the rest of the bullets off the table, but since he couldn't see anymore, he couldn't find them.

We took the gun away from him while he screamed, "Where's the ammo, where's the ammo?" I'll never forget what happened next—the guy grabbed onto the bottom of my pant leg as hard as he could. I looked down as he raised his head up and pleaded, "Please shoot me." I told him I couldn't do that, and gently took his hands off my leg and helped him lay down.

"Please help me. I can't live like this," he cried.

That wasn't the worst of it. When I told his wife what happened, she actually hit me in the chest while yelling, "Why didn't you let him kill himself? Why did you leave him that way?" She was outraged. "Why did you stop him? What the hell is wrong with you?"

That's the kind of stuff you have to live with, and it was Christmas Eve.

Sgt. John Holthusen, Minneapolis MN Police Dept.

*

Nineteen-year-old Moshe Pergament was spotted driving erratically by a Nassua County, New York police officer, who pulled over the college student's car. As the officer exited his patrol vehicle, Pergament got out of his car and approached the officer with what appeared to be a firearm. Despite the officer's repeated pleas for him to drop the weapon, Pergament continued to advance. Faced with the prospect of his own impending death, the officer fired three times, killing Pergament.

Only later did the officer learn the brutal truth: the weapon wielded by the suspect was nothing more than a toy gun. Within Pergament's car was an envelope addressed 'To the officer who shot me.' Inside was a Hallmark card with a personal inscription which read: 'Officer, it was a plan. I'm sorry to get you involved. I just needed to die. Please remember that this was all my doing. You had no way of knowing. - Moe Pergament.'

     Officer Dean Scoville, Los Angeles CA Sheriff's Dept.

*

It was a few minutes after roll call and still dark outside when I got the call a little after seven in the morning. The complaint was on a domestic violence and trespass. Officers on the night shift had been to the residence three or four times earlier, but the offender, a guy in his early twenties, kept running away whenever they arrived.

While en route to the address, dispatch advised me the subject had stated that the police were going to have to kill him. Whenever you hear that, it kinda changes the rules of the game, you know. I remember running over possible scenarios in my mind as I pulled into the long driveway that ran up to the house. I recognized the place immediately; I'd been there before on juvenile problems.

As I drove to the end of the driveway, I spotted the guy about 75 yards away, standing in a corner of the yard next to a fence. I put my cruiser in park, turned the bright lights on him and stepped out.

He started walking towards me as soon as I cleared the doorway. He had a hooded sweatshirt on, with the hood pulled up over his head. I stopped a few feet in front of the cruiser when I noticed that I could see his right hand, but not his left. Since it was dark, it was difficult to know if it was just the way he was walking, or if he was keeping his hand behind him to hide something. I yelled "show me your left hand" several times, but he just kept coming with his head down, moving faster with each step.

When he was about 30 yards away, he yanked the hand out from behind his back. In it was a long object. At first I thought it was a stick, until he started swinging it back and forth like a baseball bat. The *whooshing* sound it made as he swung it, and the reflection coming off it told me it was a metal pipe.

I drew my firearm and started backpedaling towards the cruiser while yelling over and over for him to drop the pipe. In my 13 years on patrol, I've had to draw and lock in a sight picture three, maybe four times without having to fire. For some reason, and I can't really explain why, this one had a different feel to it. Maybe it was the way he was swinging the pipe. Whatever it was, I knew he was intent on having an altercation, one way or another.

I'd been holding my gun in the low-ready position, where it's pointed just off-target and downward. By the time he got to within 30 feet of me, I raised the gun and fired one round at him. He immediately grabbed the right side of his face, then brought his right hand down in front of him and stared at it for several seconds, as if checking to see if there was any blood.

I was now back behind the left door of the cruiser. I quickly reached inside and punched the lock-release button that secured my shotgun. Just when the rack holding it fell open, he started coming towards me again in a slow trot. I leaned back over the door frame and yelled several more times for him to stop and drop the pipe.

That's when he started raising the pipe over his head, like somebody with an axe getting ready to chop wood. He was now no more than 15 feet away from me. I raised my gun again, lined my front sight over his torso and squeezed off three rounds in quick succession. He went stiff and fell face first, like a tree falling in slow motion. His hands never even came up to brace the fall. I took a deep breath to steady my nerves, and keyed the collar mike.

"Shots fired. Subject down. Need to get medical en route."

The whole thing felt unreal. It was like time slowed down, then sped back up. It was strange. I never heard my gun fire and never felt the recoil. All I saw was the bright flame from the muzzle flash. If you've never fired a .40-caliber handgun, let me tell you it packs some power, and it'll make your ears ring if you're not wearing hearing protection. Mine never did.

The screaming from the house jolted me back to reality. Somewhere around the edge of my consciousness, I knew the screaming had been going on since I fired the first shot, but I wasn't really aware of it. All my senses had blocked out everything except the threat in front of me and nothing else had registered. It was like I had blinders on. Tunnel vision.

I looked down at the body in front of me, and froze when I saw him suddenly sit up. I couldn't believe what I was seeing. I remember thinking that Superman really existed and wasn't just a comic book character after all. *Nobody* takes three center mass shots at close range and gets back up.

I yelled for him to stay on the ground, that medical was coming. He looked at me, glanced up to where his girlfriend was shouting out the window, then hopped to his feet. Like a rabbit sprinting across a yard, he took off and jumped the fence behind him.

There wasn't time to think about what had just happened. I chased him about 500 yards, through a field and an area of barns and houses. He jumped another fence and ran around a house. I followed, then broke off towards the opposite side of the structure, hoping to catch him in the middle. When I turned the corner behind the house, he was gone. Vanished—just like the ghost I was sure he was.

By this time additional units had arrived. My lieutenant went back to where the initial confrontation occurred and picked up the pipe. Shaking his head, he motioned me to come over. On one end of the pipe were three marks from where my bullets had struck, all within a small group.

No way, I thought. *No way I could've done that. That only happens in the movies...*

When I raised my pistol up, all I saw was the gun's front sight centered on his chest. I did exactly what officers are trained to do—just use the front sight when reaction time and distance are short. Somehow, I'd hit the small end of the pipe that was below his hands and in front of his chest when he raised the pipe over his head. That section of pipe was the only thing between him and my rounds, and that's what kept him alive. So how'd I hit a moving pipe in low light all three times? An act of God, maybe.

Over the next 90 minutes, the entire area of barns and outbuildings was searched in an attempt to locate him. Finally, he was spotted while trying to sneak out of a hiding place in one of the barns. He was taken into custody and charged with vandalism, domestic violence and aggravated assault on an officer. In booking, he told me that the first round went through his hair, just missing his face.

"After that, didn't you realize you were going to get killed if you came after me again?" I asked.

"Didn't care," he replied.

He served nine months before release and soon after moved back home to California. About three months later, on New Year's Eve, officers in Riverside responded to a disturbance call from a residence. When they arrived, the guy I'd shot at was there. He came at the officers with a knife. This time, there wasn't a pipe to deflect any bullets. He was shot and killed.

Would I classify this as a suicide by cop? Yeah, in his state of mind, I would. Although he didn't make any suicide threats to me, he was upset that the momma of the girl he'd been seeing in Tennessee didn't want him to see her juvenile daughter anymore. They even testified against him at his trial.

Like he told me, he just didn't care anymore what happened to him.

For some time, I kept going over and over the events in my mind. Played arm-chair quarterback on myself. Was I scared? Oh yeah, only a fool wouldn't have been. Any cop that says they're not scared in a similar situation is a liar. The guy could've easily taken my head off, and I almost took a man's life, which is the last thing any cop wants to do. But still, you've got to have the frame of mind that you'd be willing and able to take a life if needed in order to survive yourself and go home.

Finally, I realized that there wasn't anything I could have or should have done different. I had to ask myself many times if I'd hesitate to pull the trigger again if needed. The answer was always no. I wound up putting the situation behind me, so it wouldn't affect the job I have to do whenever I put on my uniform. Maybe if I'd been the one that killed him, it would've affected me different.

I've just decided not to dwell on it, because there are too many *if*'s in this job as it is.

Sgt. Shawn Franks, Jonesborough TN Police Dept.

(According to a Riverside Police Department press release dated 2/02/03, during the preliminary investigation officers were told that on past occasions the subject had made statements that "he wanted to be killed by the police." When officers arrived on the scene of the complaint, the subject was holding a knife to a child's throat. The officers ordered him to drop the knife several times, but he refused. While still holding the child, the subject charged towards the officers in an aggressive and threatening manner. One officer fired his duty weapon and struck the subject, causing a fatal injury.)

*

Some guys you think are just nutcases. I got along with this one guy particularly well, even though he didn't get along well with law enforcement at all. He got all lit up one night—drunk—and became very suicidal. He holed up in his house and called the police, making threats.

Our guys responded and some shots were fired out of the house. A standoff ensued all night. I was sleeping and at about 6:00 in the morning, I got a call to come in because the guy was asking to talk to me. So I got there and within five minutes I had him out. Not that I necessarily did something drastic; he just wanted to end it.

When he started to sober up, he realized what was going on and that he didn't trust anymore he was going to get out of there all right. But that was part of his sobering up. Earlier in the evening he was very intent on suicide by cop. We know that because when we got him out, we went to the various windows and in each one he had shotguns and ammunition lined up on the windowsill. All the shot had been removed, but the gunpowder was still in the shells. So, what he was doing was firing out the window with a big bang. It wasn't going to hurt anybody, but he was going to try and elicit fire from us to kill him. Our guys held their fire all night.

Ofc. Jack Corey, Eau Claire WI Police Dept.

*

We were on our way to lunch—this is the way police work goes—and this call comes out that a man is holding a woman hostage in a room at a local hotel. As leader of the tactical team, I started coordinating with other units on the way over. When we pulled into the hotel, the manager came running out. "I went in to talk to this guy and he pulled a gun on me," he said. "There's this girl in the room and they just jumped out the back window and drove away in a red van."

I gave out the vehicle description he provided and took off down the street. There were three of us, two in my unmarked unit and one in a marked car. We soon located the suspect's vehicle, and let the marked unit take lead in the pursuit. The speed limit is 45, but the van's going 50 or 55. Initially, he wasn't driving like a maniac, but we did see him waive the gun around so we knew he still had it.

When we got by K-Mart, he drove over the curb and went down the service road on the south side of the street. Another squad car came up and maneuvered around a huge pile of snow blocking the road. It got to the point where there was no place else to go. The deputy got out of his vehicle to approach, but the guy drove over the hump of snow and almost flipped the van over. Everyone else got stuck behind, but I was able to stay with him as he headed back onto the highway.

We soon approached a red light at an intersection where traffic was gathered. I told the other units that I thought we'd have him boxed in. Well, he jumped over the median and started going up the adjacent highway in the wrong direction. As a semi came around the curb towards him, he jumped over the median again and turned south on another highway. I crossed over and followed him in time to see he'd blown a tire out. Now he's driving on the rim with one tire. He's not really going that fast, but he just won't stop and there's a gun and the girl in the car. That's all we know—he was holding a hostage. That's what we were told.

As he's getting closer to the mall, we knew once he got into the parking lot with a gun and all the people around, we were going to be in trouble. That's when we decided to do a pursuit intervention technique. If you come up on a vehicle from behind and hit it on the rear corner, all you have to do is just push on it and their car will spin right out. If you stay with it, they will spin out and their engine will kill. Well, when I came in and made contact, he spun around and started to turn a little sideways, so I didn't push him any more. He ended up sliding sideways into a ditch, but came right back out. Even though he had no front tire, he's still driving like this. I did the maneuver three times and on the third time, just before he got to the mall, he went through the median and turned north. Now, he's coming back into the city.

I got on the radio and told the deputy chief that we're going to have to stop this guy. I said that I was going to take him right into the ditch and try to hold him there so he can't get out. I waited until we were past the approaching steep drop at an overpass because I didn't want him to roll off that. Just beyond, I did the maneuver again. As he spun around, I made contact with the front of his vehicle, causing his engine to die. We both stopped less than 10 feet apart.

Another squad car pulled up next to him and started giving him orders to get out of the car. He just turned around and pointed the gun at himself. *If you're going to shoot yourself, there's nothing I can do about that*, I thought. All of a sudden he shifted his position and the girl started to reach over. I thought he was going to kill her and then kill himself. So that's when I started shooting. I ended up hitting him maybe five times in the chest and another officer next to me with a shotgun hit him with a slug one time. As soon as I saw him slump forward, we stopped shooting and went over to pull him out. An ambulance had been following us, so they pulled up and took him to the hospital. He didn't survive.

All this happened around noontime. By the time we finished writing the reports and statements, and had been interviewed several times, it was about 5 or 6:00. My wife wasn't due home until a little later and I planned on doing some shopping at a local department store that day. When I got done at work I thought I might as well go over there. While I was in the store, I could hear people saying, "Did you hear about the shooting?" It just became surreal, almost like I was sitting there and watching a movie. I said to myself, *you know, you were just involved in a shooting and you just don't go shopping after something like that*. It was a strange feeling. I turned around and left. It was just too weird.

What's it supposed to be like after you've been involved in a gun battle? Can you tell me? Well, I don't know either. It just seems like there should be something. But it was just an everyday routine. You're back to, "Okay, I just shot somebody. Let's go out for supper tonight." So it was pretty strange. I can't say I didn't go through anything, because everybody does. You're going to in any traumatic event.

You've gotta rationalize it to yourself to some degree. People have asked me, "I bet you're really pissed at this guy," and I've said, "No, I feel sorry for him." He obviously had things going on in his life and had threatened suicide before, the family told us. In fact, he'd threatened to do what we call suicide by cop. He threatened to kill his family and had said, "The cops are going to have to come and shoot me. I'm going to make the cops shoot me."

It's something he wanted to do and it's unfortunate that all of us got stuck in the middle of his problem. He had his choices. He had ample opportunity and I know I did everything I could. All I could do was watch him act and I reacted. It's unfortunate it turned out that way. It was bad. It was uncomfortable. I've lost some sleep over it, but life has got to go on.

Lt. Karl Fisher, Eau Claire WI Police Dept.

6

THE HEAVY WEIGHT
OF THE THIN SHIELD

"Off duty, I'll walk out to my car at night and always find myself looking around. Are any cars running? Are people sitting in cars? Do all the cars have frosted windows except that one? There isn't any other job that makes you start thinking like that."

Whether you're struggling with a minimum wage job or banking six figures, stress can be an unwelcome work companion, gnawing at your senses while scraping its sharp nails across your mental chalkboard. It might just be an occasional irritation, like the fleas causing a Bluetick Hound to scratch itself on a hot summer afternoon, or it can be as constant as the infomercials on television after midnight.

The stress associated with law enforcement is somewhat unique when considering the impact it has on individuals. The life expectancy of a cop ranges 10 to 15 years less than the average person, and according to research appearing in *Medical News Today*, police officers have a higher incidence of strokes, heart attacks and other cardiovascular diseases than the general population, much of which can be attributed to the lifestyle associated with policing.[11]

Besides the varying shift work and its negative effects on sleep patterns, the inherent risks associated with enforcing the law and the frequency of grabbing a handful of artery-clogging fast-food between calls, this shortened lifespan may also be linked to the very essence of street patrol: periods of calmness followed by sudden moments of extreme stress. There is an abundance of medical evidence suggesting that frequent, unanticipated jolts of stress have detrimental effects on overall health.

Numerous stress hormones are released when cops experience an adrenaline burst during critical calls, and the constant dumping of these hormones into the circulatory system can wreck havoc on all the major body systems. Over time, the over-production of stress hormones can physically wear down the toughest officers. As such, cops will seek a variety of outlets to release tension…some as long-term solutions and others for short-term relief.

The methods by which officers cope with stress can be a sensitive area to explore. Not only does it reveal a personal side that many prefer to shield from the public, but going on-record with comments of how they handle stress can put individuals in a position of having to defend themselves to both their supervisors and the general public. To provide an opportunity for officers to disclose their thoughts without fear of reprisal, names have been left off the comments included within this chapter.

I think when I first started, I coped with stress the wrong way, which was joking around about it and if it was really bugging me, then drinking too much. I was involved in a situation where an officer was killed. I was there in the next yard when he was shot and killed, and helped carry his body into another yard and did CPR on him. He was shot a couple of times in the head and chest. It was a horrible thing to deal with; I didn't know how to cope with it, so I'd drink myself to sleep. Part of the problem was I didn't feel like I could talk to my wife at the time. We're divorced now, and I'm remarried. My current wife is a cop, too.

I have no problem understanding why officers do drink to kill the pain, or have problems in their personal relationships because there are things that'll haunt you whether you admit it or not. There were times when I'd come home from work and there'd be something that happened or something I saw and not want to expose my ex-wife to it. I just shut down and didn't say anything. I was this ball of nerves and adrenalin that built up all day long from foot chases or car chases and fights. All of a sudden, you're expected to go home and kind of shift gears and you've still got all this adrenalin built up in you. All these things that you want to talk about, but you don't want to expose your loved ones to, so you just shut down. Then when little things irritate you or whatever, you explode or shut down further.

I think at the time I didn't decompress. I just walked around constantly under pressure and with all these chemicals in my system. At the time I wasn't working out or doing healthy activities. I think now I've found a lot more healthy ways. I have a boat and we go fishing. The kids go tubing. I snow mobile. There are a lot of things I do to reduce stress now. I work out three or four times a week; that helps tremendously. And now I think when stressful things happen to me, it's easier to deal with because I'm not compounding on top of stuff that's already bottled up.

*

A wise sergeant in the Army told me, "The United States Army will be here tomorrow, the next day and the next day, and the next year and 10 years from now, whether you're in it or out of it. The Army will still continue to roll. The Army will take everything you have to offer, including your family, if you let it. Do not give your family to the Army."

That was some of the wisest advice I ever received, and it's the same for law enforcement. Law enforcement will take everything you throw at it, including your family and your life, and you have to draw the line somewhere. That's how I deal with the stress of the job. My thing was that I was always an adrenaline junkie, so in the summer I'd mountain bike like crazy, separating my shoulder and popping my sternum out a few times. In the winter I was racing snowmobiles.

All that probably had to do with the job. You get that much adrenaline at work, you have to compensate it with playtime.

*

I make it a point to keep some friends outside the department. There are more things than just being a cop. That's why I think the average life expectancy of a police officer is 57 or 58. You've got to have outside hobbies and friends because you can't have this job alone.

I mean, if you just went day-to-day and drove around and just took your domestic calls, your 911 calls, and really didn't get too excited about anything, I think you'd be fine. But, I also think you'd live a boring life. You wouldn't be having fun, but I don't think your health would suffer either. If you go out there and do the job aggressively and have fun with it, and it excites you, it also has an effect on you, too.

*

I like to run, get some exercise. Get out and do something to relieve the stress. For eight and a half hours—and I'll tell my fiancé this and she'll never understand it and the people who aren't in law enforcement won't understand it, but for that eight and a half hours, even though a lot of us are big and macho and won't admit it, we're pretty scared at times in dealing with stuff. It's *very* scary. So much uncertainty is present in dealing with things and not knowing who you're dealing with.

During a shift, if you were to draw a straight line as far as your awareness, as far as a normal person just relaxing, if that person was in the middle, I would say we're almost double that because of the stress level. And when you have to draw a bead on someone with your firearm, it's not something you recover from right away. You have your adrenalin rush and your thoughts are racing. It's a nervous, extreme high.

What will happen for eight and a half hours is I'm so high and so aware and just so on edge that all my senses work very well. As I'm talking to you, I'm listening to the radio. I'm looking in all my mirrors, looking around, and I know what's going on. For eight and a half hours you do that. It's so tiring, so stressful that when you get home—and a lot of guys I know do this—when you get home there's the normal level and you'll drop so far below that. You'll sit home, grab the remote and click the TV, and you're asked, "Where do you want to go out for dinner? What do you want to do? Where do you want to go on vacation so we can start to plan things?" It turns into a situation where I've been making decisions for eight and a half hours, being in control, that I don't really want to make a decision at home.

"You want me to do this? I don't care. You want to go out to eat? I don't care."

*

You become addicted to it; it's a drug. You become an adrenaline junkie. I think that's what kills cops, personally. I think it's the roller coaster ride. It's incredible how you get hyped up. It's kind of a sickness in a way. You also get addicted to being needed. You get addicted to being Superman, who comes running up and saying, "I'm here to save the day." But after a while, you begin to understand how destructive that addiction is.

For the average cop, maybe two or three hours a shift is spent doing something active. The rest of the time is driving around or doing paperwork. The majority of our calls are mundane—theft calls, suspicious person calls, or the person is GOA [gone on arrival] when you get there. Most of the time the event is over with or the bad guy is gone when you arrive. But you've always got to be prepared for anything. That's why cops are on edge all the time.

*

One of the things I did to handle stress was becoming an evidence tech. They teach photography in the program so you can learn how to document crime scenes. The type of photography was taking pictures of dead bodies, fire scenes, robberies—just taking pictures of really lousy stuff. Autopsies, suicides, all kinds of bad stuff. That really gets you up close and personal to some nasty things.

So I used the photography to do other things, because the same techniques that I'd use for photos of a dead body are the same techniques you use for general photography. The techniques you use for surveillance are the same techniques used for wildlife photography and for other, less gruesome tasks. I did some wedding photography. I prefer a lot of wildlife photography; that puts me in the woods.

*

Don't take this job home with you. If you have a spouse you can talk to about stuff, tell them. It's kind of a double-edged sword. Let's say you go home and tell your wife you had a guy point a gun at you, that he missed when he fired a round, and you ran after him and tackled him to the ground. Well, your wife is thinking about how you almost got killed today. You're thinking about how cool it was, the adrenaline rush, and that you want to go back to work. She's worried about you all day long.

Then the day you don't call her like you normally do, she's thinking the worst. She turns the news on to see if you've been shot or killed. She's freaking out, wondering where you are. When it's 3:00 in the morning and you're held over because you've got a drunk driver at 2:30, she's even more freaked out because you aren't home now. That just multiplies and it becomes bigger and bigger.

Before you know it, your wife is like, "I can't deal with it because I'm afraid you're going to get killed and I can't be married to you anymore." It happens all the time. There are a lot of cop divorces, I know that for sure. Probably half of all the cops I know are divorced.

*

A cop can come on this job, male or female, it doesn't matter. They can have a perfectly normal and healthy relationship with somebody and get divorced in five years. It happens all over the place, but in police work, it's higher than almost anywhere else. And the reason is, when you talk with these cops they'll undoubtedly say, "My husband or wife doesn't understand me

115

anymore, I can't talk to them. They don't understand or respect what I do. All they're doing is bitching at me because I'm working or doing this." They don't understand why their personal life has gone to shit, because it's so subtle. It's almost sinister in a way.

I've seen a lot of guys who've retired after 20 years on the job who've done nothing but the street for the most part, and they're an empty shell. They're bitter and have no friends anymore. They're on their second or third wife, or they don't have a wife anymore because they've divorced three of them and lost half their pension. Why'd it happen to them? Because they never separated it, never got away from dealing with the shit all the time.

Historically, cops don't self-help. They just don't. It's the persona that they're supposed to be able to take care of anything. Cops aren't supposed to express any emotion; they're supposed to ball everything up inside and deal with it.

*

Yeah, I talk to my wife. I talk to her all the time about work. If I don't talk to my wife, it's not because I try to be stoic. It's just I probably forgot about it and put it in the back of my mind, or we're both just too tired when we get home to discuss things. If there's something that bothers me, absolutely I tell her. I've gotten into numerous debates with other cops about that because I know other cops who say they don't want their spouses to know anything about the job.

My feelings are if you don't tell your wife about your job, how can you expect her to have any empathy towards you? Cops always wonder why people don't support them, you know, the "you don't know about my job, you've never been in my shoes" mentality. The only way other people can ever know about the job is to either be in your shoes being a cop, or you tell them. If they're not going to become a cop and you don't tell them what it's like, of course they're not going to have any empathy. I tell my wife everything, from when I've been scared out of my mind to when I've been mad as a hornet. It's amazing. She understands.

*

I don't talk about the gore in front of my kids, but I'll tell my wife. In my opinion, the gore is what shapes your foundation. The average details of arguing with somebody or getting into a fist-fight or whatever is not that sharp of a blow to your internal psyche. What is a blow is that gore, when you look down at some guy whose head is split open and you see his brains spread on the sidewalk.

For example, I was working homicide and was over at the medical examiner's office for a post-examination of a body to see if it was a natural death or homicide. So, out comes the body bag with a two-year-old kid that looked exactly like my son. That's a tremendous blow, which I didn't show externally, but internally it affected me.

No matter how much I try to explain the gore, I don't really go into the details like, "you should have seen the chunks of brain that were imbedded in the dashboard of a car," because even then she can't visualize it because she's never seen it.

*

The sound of a human body impacting from eight or nine stories up in the air is something you never forget. It's really nasty. I remember one jumping incident where we were down below, clearing the landing zone, as it were. I was really surprised, after the guy jumped, the number of people who approached me and somehow implied, "Why didn't you guys do more? This was very hard for me to watch."

I remember looking at them and saying, "You could've walked away. Why'd you stay and watch? Now you want to make your emotional problem my emotional problem? Get the hell outta here."

*

I don't think there's anyway you can't bring it home, no matter what you do with it and what kind of things you have set up at home. I teach stress issues and deal with officers who have stress issues related to specific traumatic events, and in the education phase, we talk about how to manage stress.

I talk about the importance of having a good support system at home or whatever because there's a lot of families where the spouse and the kids don't want to hear about what's going on out there because some of it's pretty brutal, and some of it's pretty cruel and nasty stuff, and they don't want to be exposed to that. That creates a dilemma for the officer. The spouse says to "just leave that crap at work and I don't want to hear about it." But the officer has to process it somehow, so one of the problem ways to deal with it—one of the bad ways to deal with it—is that you see a lot of alcoholism or drinking problems. To a lesser degree other drug problems, but you do see drug problems in law enforcement.

Marriages frequently don't last a long time. You have to process it somehow, and one of the aggravating things in law enforcement is when you've had a particularly nasty day at work and you know for a fact your spouse has told you to never bring that stuff home. The officer is cut off at home, but still needs to deal with it. So what does he do? Goes to the tavern after work and have a couple of beers.

Police tend to go to taverns where there are more police. So you get the cop bar. Who comes to cop bars? Groupies come to cop bars. You get a lot of groupies out there. Thrill seekers. So you're sitting there talking with your buddies about what happened during the day and one of these groupies will start paying attention. They want to hear everything that you're talking about. Now you've got this sympathetic ear going, and they'll take it all in. They'll comfort you, no doubt about it. So you have a lot of booze going and you've got an infidelity situation in progress. Before you even go home, you've compounded the problem before you've even solved it. You haven't talked to anybody legitimately about it yet. Those are the kinds of things we deal with.

If you have a good, strong home life, or an agreement as to where you can settle the stress, so much the better. Cops that marry into the profession, like 911 dispatchers, EMS or other cops, seem to have spouses who understand the stressors better than those from the outside.

Exercise—you see a lot of officers involved in exercise. Fitness issues, that's as much for regular job requirements as it is for stress relief.

Beyond their own coping mechanisms, only a small percentage of cops seek professional help for personal issues; it's the 800-pound gorilla in the room few will acknowledge. "Only the weak get counseling" is a prevalent mentality in law enforcement, and this mindset relates back to the control, power and authority that comes with the badge. According to psychologist Dennis Conroy, Ph.D., a retired police officer and author of the book *Officers at Risk*, relationships and depression are the two biggest internal struggles cops face. Based on his experience, officers are an underserved population in the mental health world. The reason? Possibly because most don't trust mental health professionals, as many have had a bad experience with counseling or know someone who has. "Being a cop changes the way people see the world," explains Dr. Conroy. "They don't really see anything good being permanent; it's transient. The only things cops see on a consistent basis is the negative, so they stop really building on the positives in relationships or investing in relationships. And if you don't invest in a relationship, they don't last."

Dr. Conroy is in a unique position to offer insight on the emotional battles officers face; the majority of patients he sees in his clinical practice are cops. "[Officers] seldom see goodness, and with no goodness, there is often no hope for a brighter future. Depression isn't just sadness; it's sadness with an element of hopelessness. It's the hopelessness that is keyed off of an almost constant exposure to a negative environment," he points out.

How many times in your own life have you thought, "I've got enough of my own problems, I really don't want to hear yours?" That mindset doesn't work well in law enforcement, for a large part of the job is finding out what problems others are facing, then helping to resolve them. In effect, those in uniform are constantly shouldering their own burdens in addition to the problems of those they come in contact with. Unfortunately, when they return to the sanctuary of their homes after dealing with everyone else's problems during a shift, then isolate themselves from issues on the home front, their own relationships can spiral downhill.

At home, you are expected to be accessible, vulnerable and loving. They really don't want to hear your stories, because it either scares them or they have stories of their own. It's all relative in their mind. They come to you with problems that you don't want to hear because you just spent 8-10 hours dealing with the problems of the world. The adrenalin is gone and you're exhausted. All you want to do is be alone and disengaged. It's just another form of survival.

In some aspects, those in law enforcement represent a closed society. They generally shun the media, and can be distrusting of outsiders. Skepticism runs deep when you're constantly dealing with people who, despite being caught red-handed, will swear on their kid's lives they weren't speeding, didn't backhand their spouse or steal the pint of Jack Daniels hidden under their jacket. Half-truths and outright lies become fallback responses when expensive citations or jail time hang in the balance. As a result, trust becomes a rationed commodity with cops, both on and off duty, and is extended to relatively few people they encounter.

Many tend to find solace within their own ranks, forming a tight circle around those they do trust. The "thin blue line" actually exists (a conceptual line which denotes police are the only thing standing between law-abiding citizens and anarchy), and those who don't bleed blue are frequently kept at arms-length in social settings.

If someone outside of law enforcement could just put on a uniform and walk around, they'd be well aware of everyone watching everything they did. Staring at you, looking at you, and suddenly forming an opinion of you because you put a uniform on. You're not even a police officer, but they don't know that. As soon as you walk in somewhere, they're people who will instantly hate you and others who will want to come up and talk to you because they like you. Everybody is going to be watching everything you do. Part of it is just wearing a uniform of any kind.

The uniform, or the idea that you're a police officer—once people find out who you are in your off time—really and suddenly puts this little sign on you when you're walking around, and you become well aware of it. Because of the nature of our job, you always have to be cognizant of somebody who does become aware, like a whole restaurant that becomes aware you're a police officer. You have to say, "Is there anybody here I need to worry about?"

You don't have to do that for any other kind of job. It does make having a social life away from other police officers really, really difficult. I think anybody could put a uniform on and instantly know what I'm talking about.

It's hard to develop friends. It's not that I don't want to, but you can't find people who just won't separate the two. "This is my private life, and let's go do the things I want to do, like your other friends." I think it's difficult to have those social relationships with those outside law enforcement, but you can with other police officers. No matter where you go, I think you find you're universally accepted and taken care of, and that sort of thing.

*

Off duty, you have to be careful as a police officer in watching what you do and where you go. If I go to a bar or somewhere and have a drink or two with something to eat—or just while hanging out with some of my friends—I really don't want people to know I'm a police officer. Even though I'm doing something that normal people do, people will look at you like, "Look at that cop, what's he doing drinking a beer?"

What, is it illegal or something for me to have one?

Another situation is when people you hang around with who normally wouldn't want to have a conversation that has anything to do with the police at all, they continually crack jokes about "Don't take me to jail" or "I didn't do it" or stuff like that. That's the reason most cops wind up hanging around other cops off duty. All my friends are in law enforcement. Even the ones I hang with off duty.

*

The hard part is getting to know people and making small talk with people that aren't in law enforcement. The problem is everybody wants to hear about your job. You don't get to know other people as well because you're the one telling the stories. You spend all your time talking. I hate going to a party where maybe one or two people know you, and no one else does because they're going to tell everybody, "Yeah, he's a cop."

Then everybody is going to start asking you about stuff. Whether it's about the law or whether it's about the traffic ticket they got, or whether they want you to tell stories and stuff. A lot of times, that's when you don't want to be talking about work or dealing with it. I think that's why you get cops just hanging around other cops because they can talk about the things they want to talk about. You aren't going to have another officer saying, "Well, what's this with police chases? Why do the cops chase people? Why can't the cops shoot someone in the leg?" Then you've got to explain all that stuff, or you feel like you've got to defend some other law enforcement officer's actions. I think it's very difficult, and if you're not the kind of person that's very social anyway, it makes it even harder.

I usually end up answering the questions. I used to—and I don't do this as much anymore—if people started going too far, I'd tell them a story that would make them quit asking me questions. I'd tell them something gross and they'd say, "Okay, that's enough. Let's talk about something else." I'd talk about accident scenes or when I did CPR on a two-year-old that was shot. Pretty soon they'd quit asking me questions.

A lot of times, cops won't tell people what they do. They don't want to talk about it.

*

When I'm off duty, I think it makes me a little more paranoid with my own family. You tend to watch your wife and kids more like a hawk, like a mother hen, because you have knowledge of what goes on out there. You don't trust anyone, and at times it makes my wife ill. We'll sit in a restaurant and my back is against the wall, where I can see everything coming in and going out. I think at times it puts stress on the spouse, and a lot of times it affects the way you talk to your spouse.

As far as the general public, people have to earn my trust off-duty. Let's say you're in Wal-Mart. I don't trust anyone around me. Just for the simple fact that a rapist or killer doesn't have that stamped on their forehead. I think that having kids, and knowing what people can do to kids, you tend to be a little paranoid with your own.

As far as other personal relationships, you tend to feel more comfortable being around your own people—your fellow officers. When you're around that group, you know that everyone is safe; nobody is really going to do anything. My wife says it's hard for me to make friends because I don't trust people. It's not that I'm mentally paranoid, like a mental illness or anything. It's just when somebody walks up to you and your kid and says, "That's a pretty child you have there." I'll just say, "Thank you." Speak and go. I'm not there to be chummy. I guess that's the way it affects me a little bit.

*

My best friends are bankers. Some of my friends are in real estate. I do that on purpose. You need to keep a balance. A couple of my friends are cops. There are so many cops whose lives revolve around being a cop. Some can survive doing that. I just can't. I work twelve hours a day as a cop. I don't want to go home and watch cop shows. It's too much. I'd like to be a normal person for once.

*

It's hard to interact with some people outside of law enforcement at a party or something, because as a cop we do what other people might consider to be strange things in our career. And you really can't just talk about it because they have no concept of it at all. They've never been exposed to the things we've been exposed to.

I live in a suburb and those people, they've never seen violence in their life. They've never seen the kind of violence and crime that I've seen. So it's tough for them to even fathom it, and thus it's tough to even talk to them about it.

*

I probably have equal amount of friends in both circles. My two closest friends aren't in law enforcement, but I also have some very close friends who are in law enforcement. So, I socialize with both groups, depending on the setting. Sometimes the groups are combined.

Now, you do certain things with cops because you know they can understand some things better. The frustrations you're feeling sometimes, the cops seem to understand more than the non-cops. My friends I have outside of law enforcement were my friends before I got into law enforcement, so they've been there all along. Some of my friends—well, they've seen the cop shows, and they think that's how everything is. It's not like that, and you have to explain it to those people.

*

We need to separate work from leisure. People often don't understand that. They expect if you're a cop, you've got to be that cop 24/7. Now, should you be held to a higher standard 24/7? Sure you should, because you're a cop. You should be somebody that's respected and is a decent person. You shouldn't be out there doing stupid things.

On the other hand, I don't go to your house and ask you about your work and make you constantly discuss it when you're at home and trying to get away from the office. Please, let us get away, too.

Just as the public has difficulty in separating an officer's professional and personal lives, cops often find it hard to disconnect themselves from the law enforcement mentality away from work. Off duty, it's not unusual for them to be constantly analyzing their surroundings, evaluating who may pose a threat to them, their family, or anyone else in close proximity. For example, when stopping at a bank or convenience store, many will park where they can view what's going on inside before exiting their personal vehicle. Upon entering, they'll make quick assessments of the customers to decide if a threat is imminent, such as an armed robbery or a "smash and grab" theft.

And if they have to walk around a building, some will habitually take a wide angle around the corner (a tactical maneuver called "slicing the pie," which means for each step taken around an area with an obstructed view, a greater sight picture is gained). This provides a margin of safety should a potential threat be lurking on the other side, such as armed dopers transacting business or gang-bangers looking for easy prey.

While driving, it's not uncommon to automatically revert to the "patrol scan," where attention is split between driving and analyzing all the activity taking place within eyesight. Even a mundane task, such as walking outside to check the mailbox can elicit cautious behavior, like scanning the area for anyone nearby, or looking for any unfamiliar or occupied vehicles parked along the street.

When you're a cop, it's hard to turn off the policing mindset and relax off duty, especially when carrying a concealed firearm in a public setting. The same mindset that protects you on the job keeps your senses heightened when the uniform is still hanging in the closet.

It's what you have become, and it can be mentally exhausting.

7

POLICING THE POLICE

*"When there's an emotionally charged, angry situation,
somebody's gotta stand up and take the heat, and that's us.
We screw up and we do good things. As long as we're held
accountable, we hold ourselves accountable and are motivated by
the right things, we'll be all right. That's what makes us different
than a lot of other places."*

As any good defense attorney will incessantly point out to those
seated in a jury box, there are established standards which must
be followed when it comes to protecting the rights of alleged
offenders. And there should be, for people do get falsely accused
and imprisoned for crimes they didn't commit; DNA analysis has
proven that in a number of cases. But there is a sentiment among
those in law enforcement that society sometimes dismisses the
victim's rights, as well as the rights of officers. When any of these

groups don't receive equal weighing on the scales of Lady Justice, the whole criminal justice system becomes questionable.

Whenever a cop straps on their gear and steps out in public, they're placed on a petri dish and closely scrutinized under a microscope by the public eye. And the moment trouble erupts, society expects officers should react quickly to whatever situation they confront, and should do everything appropriately. In a perfect world, this would happen. However, in the world we've been given to work with, cops are imperfect human beings and can make mistakes when thrust into highly stressful situations with rapidly changing dynamics.

When the pressure is on, do you normally need a minute to compose yourself and think about your options, or maybe to call someone else for guidance? Not going to happen in this line of work; when a situation suddenly turns violent, you have to react immediately, and as the threat changes, adapt to it without hesitation. Anything less risks personal injury or injury to someone else. Even so, many citizens have little tolerance for error, and completely disregard the fact some decisions must be made faster than a professional athlete denying steroid use.

When you have to make quick choices that will significantly impact someone else's life, second-guessing is inevitable. And it's not just the public playing arm-chair quarterback, analyzing each step of the decision-making process. It's the officer as well, who may find themselves experiencing the *shoulda, coulda, woulda* moments while replaying the scenario over and over, long after the dust has settled.

"I look at all the situations in my career, and I've done some dumb stuff. Every cop has who's ever been on the job for any length of time. We've all done stuff you'd say you'd never do. Maybe slammed a guy to the ground too hard, or maybe threw a guy across a room. There's times you lose your cool and do stuff. You look at the Rodney King situation. I don't justify it, but I can see how it happened. Or a kid who gets punched in the mouth on the back of a squad car in handcuffs. I can see how that happens, and I can explain to you how that happens, because I've been in situations where you lose your cool.

The average Joe doesn't understand it because they've never been in a situation where they've been so afraid—or so mad—with the adrenaline flowing and you have to fix the problem, make the scene safe because it's not safe yet. That's when you make the mistakes where you make it safe the wrong way. Most cops can understand why these things happen. It doesn't make it right; we've all been there, done that. It's just reality, and that's a problem. That's why it's very hard for cops to police their own, because on that next call, you might be the one scrutinized.

The other side of it is that we get falsely accused of many, many things. I'll be the first to say I've done some wrong things, some dumb things, but not criminal things. If I had the chance to do some things over again, hell yeah, I'd do them different. But then again, I would've had the time to think about it, the time to make a decision.

Part of the problem is we have people analyzing us who don't understand the split-second decisions that have to be made out there. How many jobs can you name where people have to make split-second decisions every day? What's really bizarre about this job is you never know how something is going to end until it's over. If you think you can predict how it's going to end, you're in trouble. If you think one domestic is going to be like the last one—well, that's what kills cops."

Anonymous

"Cops pay a hell of a price to be able to create the persona that they can handle any situation thrown at them. It's just not human to be able to do everything. I look at the people that always want to second guess what we do. Don't get me wrong, they have a right to do that because we're public servants who are given a lot of power, a lot of responsibility. But we are also human beings who sometimes make mistakes. We should be critiqued, because if we make the same mistakes over and over and don't learn from them, we have a real problem.

What's frustrating to me is people will take weeks—and sometimes months—to analyze and critique the actions of someone who had maybe a half-second to make a decision. Sometimes I would love to say to them, 'Okay, you've got a half-second to analyze and critique. Go!'

That's why we rely heavily on training and supporting one another. It's the old thin blue line you've heard of. It's true. Is it right? Sometimes, sometimes not. But is it necessary? Yes, to some degree. We certainly shouldn't cover up any criminal activity by officers. But we need people in our lives that understand what we do for a living, and to be supported by them.

I've given up trying to justify why police officers do what we do. All you can do is to try to explain it, and hope people understand and care."

Sgt. John Holthusen, Minneapolis MN Police Dept.

Accusations against officers are a common occurrence; it's the nature of the job. Being in a position of authority, they usually have an adversarial encounter with the people they come in contact with, and that's the seed from which many complaints grow. Still, a sizable portion of grievances don't always involve wrongdoing by an officer, but instead the complainant simply dislikes what's being done. Usually, those complaining the loudest are either getting arrested or involved in some type of unlawful activity—the very people who don't like the police in the first place. The average citizen doesn't call in often, since they have little contact with law enforcement.

A common scenario is when someone phones in and complains an officer called them a jerk, or some other descriptive term with a little more shock-value. They've not committed a crime by any means, but there's an expectation, both departmentally and publicly, that cops should always act professional, regardless of the type of insults or threats directed towards them. But it's often difficult; again, they're human and can lose their temper like anyone else. How would you react if someone insinuated they're going to find out where you live, track down your wife and kids and wait until you're not home to get even? What would you do if you got sucker-punched after stepping between a spouse and their abusive partner? One way or another, it's going to have an effect on you.

Accountability is a term frequently attached to virtually all police activities. Cops make an arrest to hold someone accountable for their actions. The legal system holds the officer accountable for the methods used in the arrest, and the public holds the police department accountable for enforcing the law. If everyone does their part as required, the law enforcement machine runs as designed. But if one part malfunctions, then problems begin to roll downhill until they land on top of some blue shirt at two in the morning.

"If we're going to be held to artificially high standards, then everyone else should be, too. I'll give you an example. Loud party goes sour when I'm working midnights on the poor side of town. And during the party, somebody gets pushed through a window. They lead with both hands and go right through the glass. When they're pulled back in, they're cut like ribbon candy from their elbows to their fingertips.

One of the people there grabs a jizz-stained bed sheet and wraps the guy's arms up in it. He's bleeding badly, so the paramedics arrive to take him to the hospital. It's chaos in the street; the party is going on with fighting and people yelling at the cops trying to clear the crowd.

The last thing the medics do before leaving is drop this blood-soaked sheet on the street and drive away. Now, what the hell am I supposed to do with it? So we leave, and immediately the phone starts ringing at the precinct. 'I can't believe you guys left that in the middle of the street like that. It's a hazard. You come out here and take it away right now!'

Well, we didn't leave anything anywhere; it was the ambulance service. And, I don't have at two in the morning the ability—how the hell am I even gonna dispose of it? So, I grab a garbage bag from the precinct, put on a pair of rubber gloves, go out there and put the bed sheet in the bag. I tie it up tight and drive around until I find some closed business not near any residences and throw it in their dumpster. I'm still causing a hazard, since someone could find that and get infected.

So, I call the ambulance supervisor and made them drive all the way in from outside the county. I told the supervisor that I didn't want to get the guys in trouble, didn't want to know their names, but he needed to talk with them and tell them that's bullshit, cause they're the ones set up to dispose of hazardous stuff, not us. But still, the phone rang and we got blamed—the police—not for something we did, but for something you did. I'll bear all the blame for something we did, but not for something somebody else screws up.

My final comment was, 'I bet you fifty bucks that bed sheet wouldn't have landed in the street if that call was in a higher class neighborhood.' He agreed."

Anonymous

In many cities, the police department is the main source of stories the local news media covers. As such, the media naturally focuses on departmental activities, and sometimes even assumes a watchdog role to "police the police." But what makes the news isn't always a complete account of the events surrounding a story. Incidents worthy of coverage often involve complex situations with many variables, making it difficult to accurately summarize them with a couple of column inches in a newspaper or a 15-second blurb on television. Still, news reporting tends to shape public opinion, and because the media may be the only source of information the public receives about a police action, it's their version of events most will remember.

With the constant media coverage of law enforcement activities coupled with the public's fascination of police work, every cop out there knows for every action they take, for whatever itch they scratch, there's a good chance they'll be scrutinized by someone. Like a deer hunter who accidentally walks into a PETA convention, they're going to be the center of attention, like it or not. That's why during street patrol, the "momma test" (would you say or do that in front of your mother?) becomes the "media test" (would you say or do that in front of a camera?). On any call, there's always a chance whatever they do will be recorded by someone, be it a film crew or some individual toting a camcorder or cell phone. For many officers, this consideration can't be ignored when brute force must be utilized.

"I tackled a guy one night who wrecked his car behind a factory in the middle of nowhere. We got to wrestling around and I wound up getting the best of him. Just as soon as I got one handcuff on, I felt my holster unsnap. He had gotten a hold of my holster, unsnapped it and was pulling my pistol forward. I grabbed the pistol and got it back in, but it was a tug of war. He'd already grabbed it and it was coming out. I ended up hitting him really, really hard with my free hand, and the fight was over. That was the only time that's ever happened, and let me tell you, it's a bad feeling.

The people who watch a video of something like this wind up screaming 'police brutality, police brutality!' They don't know what it's like to get into a fight with somebody and you're trying to handcuff them while getting hit and spit on, and you know if the guy gets away from you, they're going to try and hurt you or somebody else. On top of that, your adrenaline is wide open.

How many people get into a fist fight with someone and they completely keep their attention on doing exactly what they're supposed to do? It doesn't always happen that way. People think we're super-human or believe we can just slam someone down on the ground and handcuff them and everything is okay. It's just not easy to arrest somebody who wants to fight with you. It's not pretty."

Sgt. Eddie Graybeal, Washington County TN Sheriff's Office

"Had a shots fired call; an Asian male was seen in the alley firing a gun. Me and another squad meet at the end of this alley. Sure enough, there's an Asian male, hands in his pockets. Skinny, small guy, about 5' 3" and probably 120 pounds. We grabbed him and put him on the car, but he wouldn't take his hands out of his coat pockets. I had one arm, another cop had the other arm, and another cop had his gun pushed right up against his head.

We pulled his hands out a little bit, and he had a .357 in one hand and a .45 in the other hand, fingers on the triggers. It seemed like it took forever and all the while we're screaming, 'We're going to kill you! We're going to kill you!' I can't remember to this day how we got the guns out of his hands, but we didn't have to shoot him. He was locked onto those damn guns—wouldn't take his hands off them. I'm sure we were punching him, hitting him, and just beating him to make him loosen up on those guns.

But then, how would that have looked to the media? Put a round in his head, and he's got two guns in his pockets. And I'm thinking while we're dealing with him, how bad it's going to look if we have to shoot this guy in the back of the head. Here we are, a squad car and three cops, and crap like that's running though your head. He's got two guns in his hands, and you're worrying about what's going to happen in the media or being sued.

So, you can't second-guess what you're doing; it has to be instinctive. Had one of those guns gone off, he would have certainly been killed. Absolutely."

Anonymous

And finally, one of the most frustrating accusations officers face is one the public, specifically parents, assumes is benign and funny in the same breath. It's when an adult tells a young child in the presence of an officer, "They put bad little kids in jail, and if you don't behave, they'll take you there, too."

What kind of impression does that leave with their wide-eyed offspring? To fear the police, of course. *Cops and the boogeyman are tag-team buddies, and they're coming to get you.*

Granted, most young kids have no conception of what jail is really like, but they're smart enough to understand it's a strange place where an intimidating person in uniform will take them, and they'll be separated from their parents. All in all, not the kind of adventure they want to be a part of.

Wouldn't parents rather have their kids respect the police, to trust them enough to call 911 if they needed help? Do they want a child to be so scared of going to jail that if they ever got lost in the woods or separated from their parents in a crowded mall, they'd be afraid to approach the officers searching for them?

It happens, and the result isn't always a story with a happy ending.

Sometimes, cops just have to bite their tongues when asinine comments like these are spoken by the very people they took an oath to protect and serve. Still, like trimming off a hang-nail with a table saw, they're going to leave a mark.

"I went to a house to help somebody retrieve some property. They had a dispute and left, and were going back to get their belongings. A little boy answered the door, probably three or four-years-old. I started talking to him, and he was talking friendly to me. We were just having a little conversation when the father walked up and yelled at the kid.

'What the hell are you doing? I told you that you can't talk to the police! The police are bad! Don't you ever trust the police!' He chastised the kid and sent him away. He looked at me and demanded to know what I wanted. I told him, and then asked him why he said that to his kid.

'Because I don't want my kid trusting the police. They'll just do you over and do you wrong.'

So, we had this discussion and it turned into me getting mad. I told him if the police are bad, then why not let his kid find out for himself. There's no need to teach him. Then I asked him if I was there to screw him over. No, I wasn't. I told him that this person wanted their property and I'm here to make sure nobody gets hurt. But it didn't matter, they don't listen. I'm the bad guy. All police are bad. And that gets passed on to the next generation."

Sgt. Steve Wickelgren, Minneapolis MN Police Dept.

8

IT'S ONLY FUNNY
IF YOU UNDERSTAND IT

"Cops have to have a sense of humor.
It may be a gallows sense of humor, and it often times is.
But it's a coping mechanism, and it's genuine."

When faced with some of the most horrible sights imaginable, officers generally have two choices: let the carnage cause severe psychological distress, or view gruesome events in a way to keep from mentally shutting down. If they plan on spending any significant amount of time on the job, they'll gravitate towards the latter option to keep their mental health from deteriorating. So, while they're powerless to change the tragic circumstances they must confront, they do have some ability to control how they process these atrocities.

Most individuals come into law enforcement without prior experience of dealing with murder victims, mangled bodies at traffic crashes or suicides where a corpse has been left hanging in a hot attic for several days. The average person might be exposed to events like these once or twice in their lives, but for cops, confronting the macabre is a frequent occurrence. The first time they deal with a particularly horrific situation, it can shock the conscience and be extremely difficult to process. However, as they are repeatedly exposed to these types of incidents over time, many will develop—by necessity—a coping mechanism known as a gallows sense of humor.

Many people aren't comfortable hearing this morbid, dark style of humor. Some even say gallows humor is inappropriate and label those who use it as insensitive. Still, it has an essential role in some settings, and that's to provide an outlet—a means of detachment—from the emotions normally experienced during horrible circumstances. Emotions that, if allowed to be felt or acted upon in typical fashion, would hinder cops from being able to perform their jobs.

Morbid humor isn't unique within law enforcement. It's frequently shared by those involved with any type of emergency services, such as EMS, firefighters and trauma physicians. And though it's often misunderstood by those outside these professions, those within know sometimes you have to make light of the darkness to preserve your own mental health while functioning on the job.

"I remember a guy who was shot in the face as he was filling up at a gas pump. Guy falls on the ground and his eyeballs blow out of his head. One of the sergeants walked up with some of the rookies and says, 'Yeah, guns are all fun and games until somebody's eye gets knocked out.'

It's a coping mechanism, a detachment. But you tell somebody about it and they say, 'You sick bastard. No, it's not.' We have our feelings like anyone else, but at some point humor has got to break in. If you don't get that humor in there, it will destroy you. This job will flat out destroy you. Everything you stand for will change at what you see. The cop is the first at the scene, so you see things that break down what you know is right or wrong. You see kids that have been sodomized; you see people that have been beaten so bad, their bones are deformed and broken. You see heads blown apart. So if you don't joke about it, it can destroy you inside. It might destroy you anyway. You need to be able to joke about it."

Anonymous

*

"You see cops use humor all the time; it's so essential. In a departmental setting it can be seen as so inappropriate, but you have to combine humor with the job or go crazy. For those outside law enforcement it could be considered shocking, but if they really thought about it, they could probably understand the need for it.

One time a female cop went to a DOA. The person had been dead for some time. He had a German Shepherd that'd eaten part of the body, and was walking around the house with some of it in his mouth. Although it would be shocking to some people, we were like, 'Come here, come here, boy.' It's like we were trying to trick the dog into dropping whatever it was. You know, 'Drop the leg, drop the leg, good boy! Now give me the hand...'

I can tell my friends outside of law enforcement about the incident, but I won't tell them about the humor we found in it because they wouldn't understand that part. It helps not taking all the bad stuff too seriously, kind of blocking it off."

Anonymous

*

"We had a coroner call. Sad situation involving a guy sitting at a table who'd been eating; he was slumped over with a green bean sticking out of his mouth. The family wasn't there when we walked in, so I looked at one of the newer officers and said, 'Hey, you had lunch today?'

He said, 'No, why?'

I pointed at the deceased guy and said, 'You want some green beans?'

Well, he went outside and threw up.

It's the kind of humor you've gotta have because you deal with so much terrible stuff. It's a release mechanism. You've gotta have a release mechanism in order to keep from hurting yourself or losing it out here. I've worked suicides involving people I grew up with, all through childhood and high school, and that's devastating. You've gotta have some way to get through that."

Anonymous

*

"I remember a guy laying there, died of a heart attack. He was in his forties, and his brother and nephew were in the same house. He'd only been dead a couple of hours but during that time their Pit Bull ate half his face off. So we got a call there for a potential homicide.

When I walked in, you could see through his throat and jaw. His left eyelid was gone, as were his nose and lips. I found humor in the fact that he had an olive drab green shirt on with the Marine Corps anchor, the ball and eagle on there. And written on the shirt was, 'The pain is temporary, but pride is forever.' Looking at the shirt, I couldn't help but laugh. Pain may be temporary and pride forever, but geez, that's gotta hurt, cause his face was eaten off! I chuckled when I said it, and one of the other officers motioned his head towards another room—in earshot—where the guy's brother and nephew were.

Yeah, I found some humor in that, but what are you gonna do? It's a coping mechanism."

Anonymous

*

"I had one guy who hung himself in an apartment complex. I was working homicide and my partner was a heavy-set fellow. So, I call out to the other officers from the third floor, 'Hey guys, we've got a dead body up here.'

'Well, yeah...we can smell it down here on the first floor,' someone yelled back.

We get the door open and you can see a foot inside the door. We could only get the door open a little bit because he'd hung himself by the air conditioner vent above the floor. Now, who's gonna go in there, me or the heavy-set partner?

He looks at me and says, 'Damn, I'm not gonna fit in there. You'll have to do it.'

'What do you mean, it stinks in there!' I said.

So, we argue back and forth until I wind up pushing the door open and there's this person who's been deceased for a week. Their head looks like a shrunken head, because all the fluids have seeped out of it. His fingers looked like Polish sausages with all the settled fluids and his skin looked like water balloons. It was like a stinkin' horror movie. And, did it smell in there. You could even taste it in your mouth.

I get in and swear I'm gonna kick my partner's ass when I get out. I'm trying to open the windows so I can breathe long enough to figure out if it's a suicide. I had to check the door to see if it was locked, and if it was possible somebody could have done this and such. So, as soon as I'm sliding by the door to get out, the rope broke and the body fell and ruptured, all the fluids splattering all over my feet.

I let out a shriek. I get out and we're kind of laughing, and cops are walking up and saying, 'Hey, how ya doin', you stink, man.'

Thanks, assholes."

Anonymous

*

If officers fixate on the anguish and death around them, it could paralyze them into inaction, reducing their ability to render aid or carry out the task at hand. It's been said the easy way to differentiate a fresh-from-the-academy rookie from a veteran is watching how each responds to a traffic fatality involving a large amount of internal organs being displayed externally. The veteran, having developed an iron stomach and detached demeanor over time, is the one who efficiently goes about the task at hand.

The newbie is the one tossing their cookies on the roadside.

While depressing events may evoke a morbid sense of humor, there's an abundance of lighter moments that bring a refreshing balance to the job. Sometimes, humor is a direct by-product of the mischievous nature of officers; other times, opportunity presents itself at unexpected moments.

"There was this guy who just wasn't right in the head. Always carried a Bible in his hand. Really, a strange character.

Me and my partner went to arrest him on some charges. We put him in the backseat of the cruiser and started making our way to the jail. On the way there, he said, 'Excuse me, officers. Do you care if I get down in the backseat and pray?'

We said no, we didn't mind. He could go ahead and pray all he wanted. He positioned himself in the seat and said just loud enough for us to hear, 'Dear Lord in heaven, would you please let a semi-truck come down the road and run over this car, and kill these two officers and not harm me?'"

Lt. Randy Bowers, Carter County TN Sheriff's Department

*

"You gotta have a sense of humor. We play jokes on ourselves. My one partner, I've scared him numerous times when we worked the streets. And, in turn, he did the same to me.

Like a few days ago, it was so hot they opened up the fire hydrants so kids could play in the water. Well, we saw one open so I rolled down his window and drove by in the squad car, and it blasted him with water through the open window. Darn near flipped the car; I didn't realize there was that much force from a hydrant.

Whole car smelled like skunk water afterwards, and it shorted out our computer."

Anonymous

*

"I'd just started on the force when we got a call on unknown trouble on the north end of the precinct. Call came in with screaming in the background. So we get there and listen outside, and hear arguing and yelling. I go towards the backyard and hear a big crash and glass breaking, and see what looks like a body on the back steps with two boots pointing up. So I get on the radio and put a call out for more squads...rescue, ambulance, the whole artillery.

Then this guy walks over from behind a fence about five feet away, and he can't figure out what's going on. Turns out he'd just thrown a bag of garbage out the back door and it landed perfectly on the back steps, right on top of a pair of boots.

I got a lot of grief about that afterwards."

Anonymous

*

"I'm sitting in my cruiser eating at a Taco Bell, listening to the CB I used to have in the car. While I'm eating my burrito I hear a guy come across the channel, talking to some girls who were in the parking lot across from me. He's like, 'Hey, this here's Cotton. We're leaving the club, let's hook up.'

I keep listening, and he starts saying he's got some pot and pills with him. Now, he's got my complete attention.

The girls tell him they're over at the Krystal, and to come on over. He says to them that he's driving a Dodge Omni and is heading their way. So I'm thinking, *Okay, Dodge Omni with two guys drunk, dope and pills coming my way...*

He gets over to Krystal and can't find them, so he starts yelling over the CB, 'Hey, it's Cotton. Where you all at?'

I key up the mike and said, 'We're all over here at the Taco Bell. Come on over.'

He pulls into the Taco Bell lot and right away runs over the curb, about flattening his tires. That gave me all the probable cause I needed. I stopped him, walked up to his car and got him out. He was so hammered, he could hardly stand up. I arrested him for DUI and his buddy for public intoxication. Under the car seat I found about a quarter pound of pot and in his pocket, a bunch of Xanax.

I transported him to jail, and he still hadn't figured out how I really caught him. He's just thinking it was because he ran over a curb. So, I'm booking him in and ask him if there's any other names he goes by. He says no.

'Well, what about your CB handle, Cotton?' I asked with a grin.

He turned white and a *holy crap* look ran across his face.

Best burrito I ever had that night."

 Sgt. Eddie Graybeal, Washington County TN Sheriff's Office

*

"Being a female out on the streets, there's certain guys, when you're arresting them, will get a kick out of that. They just think it's the coolest thing ever. It's all in how you handle yourself, I guess.

We had a guy we were arresting on a warrant the other day. I got into my squad car, and he's knocking on the back window, yelling and screaming. So I get out and open up the back door and ask him, 'What's up?'

'I was just wondering if you got a younger sister, you know, if I ever come back up here.'

I'm laughing and tell him no, but let him know he can call me anytime he wants.

'Really?'

'Yeah, the number's 911.'"

 Ofc. Jen Foster, Brooklyn Park MN Police Dept.

*

"I was pulling night shift at our department. It was springtime, and my allergies had been getting worse over several days. One minute it was like someone stuffed a throw rug up my nose, and the next minute, the mucus faucet was running wide open.

I'd gone by the detention center to pick up some paperwork and ran into one of the nurses. I asked her for a couple of Benadryl, hoping to stop the flow from my nose. I'd taken them before, and since they don't make me drowsy, I felt comfortable I could still work with them in my system. You know, it's kinda hard—even with a gun on your hip—to make people take you seriously when snot is dripping down your upper lip.

Anyway, the nurse dug up a couple of tablets and handed them to me. I remember thinking that they looked a little different from the ones I was used to taking, but didn't ask any questions. *Maybe they're the generic version*, I thought. So I did what any good cop would do—grabbed some water and swallowed them.

It wasn't long afterwards, maybe two or three in the morning, when I started feeling strange. I met up with another zone officer who was always sucking on hard candy during patrol. Thinking the sugar would give me an energy boost, I got a couple from him and hoped for the best.

Well, a few minutes later, I got dispatched to a domestic that had gotten physical. It's the kind of call that gets your heart beating faster and adrenaline going, but I was really chilled out as I sped down the road. Not stressed at all, just feeling good, really good. I remember watching my blue lights reflecting off the road signs I passed. *That looks pretty cool*, I thought. *Funny how I hadn't noticed that before*. Anyway, I wound up arresting the male aggressor, and was soon heading back to the detention center to book him on a domestic violence charge.

When I walked into booking, it was a mad house. Another officer had brought an arrestee in and the guy was going berserk, yelling and just causing all sorts of commotion. I slowly walked over and grinned at the guy and said, 'Hey man, just chill out, okay?'

That's when the nurse who'd given me the pills earlier grabbed me and asked, 'So, um...how are you, uh, feeling now?'

'A little tired, but pretty relaxed. All in all, not bad. Not bad at all,' I said.

That's when she dropped the bombshell on me.

'I screwed up...I'm so sorry,' she said. 'Instead of giving you the Benadryl you wanted, I accidentally gave you two Valium.'

Two Valium? No wonder I was so chilled out.

I decided to keep the medication mix-up between ourselves. She didn't need the trouble it would cause if word got to her supervisor about it, and the good citizens of my county didn't need to know they had a sedated cop with Valium pumping through his system protecting them that night."

Anonymous

*

"Me and another officer were searching a house one night where an alarm had gone off. We checked the front then went around back, where there was this deck that was up on the second level of the house. So we're walking underneath the deck, and there was a bird's nest with a bird in it, about head high. I'll never forget walking by the nest and that bird coming out of there, sounding like a helicopter leaving the ground.

I dropped down on my knees and hit the ground, wondering what had gotten a hold of me, and about peeing on myself. Watching the other officer horse laughing, then you both start laughing. There are just so many little things that happen in this line of work that turn out to be funny."

Sgt. Shawn Franks, Jonesborough TN Police Dept.

*

"Buy busts are the ultimate in short-term gratification for dope cops. They occur when you set up a deal with a crook to deliver drugs at a specified place and time, or to sell drugs in a reversal and an arrest is made at the scene.

G-Man was the case agent on a warrant service at Elmer's house, a disgusting meth and weed dealer who lived in your tax dollar subsidized housing within a little four-plex studio apartment. It had a shared kitchen and laundry room across from a covered porch for communal use of the tenants. Elmer was pushing 400 pounds, chain smoked and breathed with the assistance of oxygen. Every time I saw him, he was wearing sweat pants with the elastic stretched out showing the crack of his ass to the world, and a stained t-shirt that reflected the contents of his past several large meals. Elmer didn't have the best hygiene or housekeeping habits.

Elmer had a huge abdominal girth that allowed him to keep a wallet with ounces of methamphetamine broken into bindle bags for smaller sales, along with an additional wallet with several thousand dollars in it. We actually missed the dope wallet during his initial search, and Zatch saw him trying to get rid of it under a blanket we had wrapped around him while he was sitting in the foyer of the complex as we search the house. I got the lucky job of lifting up Elmer's wad of fat and searching for further evidence.

There were some places Elmer didn't see fit to wash on a regular basis.

Elmer decided to assist us, and called his dealer for a delivery of four pounds of marijuana and several ounces of methamphetamine. Although this operation started early in the morning, it was dark by the time the dealers showed up—standard doper time, in effect. Because it had taken some time to gain Elmer's cooperation, we sent out for food. During the waiting period, half of us were in the shared communal kitchen and the other half were in Elmer's studio apartment. Elmer was on the phone to the crook making arrangements for the dope delivery, and I was busy eating my Happy Meal while keeping an eye out for Elmer's visitors, who we got to meet and greet.

G-man's warrant covered the persons and vehicles of those who showed up since he was able to show that probable cause existed if you were going to Elmer's, you were there to buy dope, trade stolen property for dope, or provide dope to Elmer. These operations were fabulous when we had the time and could hide our presence from the outside, as we were able to recover all kinds of property, serve arrest warrants and strike fear into the hearts of dopers looking to score. You just never know who's going to answer the door at the local dope house, and when it was a cop in raid gear looking to detain and search you, things got interesting.

I'd finished my soft drink and had set it down on the counter to let the ice melt before drawing the last moisture out of the cup. It was a long day of wearing raid gear, peering through the blinds and waiting to take people down. They were coming in from every direction, even through the back yard of the complex, which made you stay alert or these folks would walk in on you and the surprise shoe would be on the other foot.

A few minutes had gone by, and I reached for my soft drink cup and took two long pulls on the straw after shaking the ice. I knew something was very wrong from the thick, gooey mess I sucked in and swallowed, but I was unable to stop before I got the second hard pull of Skoal Long Cut that had been deposited by G-Man in a very similar cup on the counter exactly where I had left mine.

I was no stranger to chew, but really never had been enamored with Skoal Long Cut, especially after sucking a couple of mouthfuls of what I thought was G-Man's chew spit. We were close, but not that close...and my Happy Meal was coming out.

I started heaving into the communal sink while Elmer was on the phone trying to negotiate the deal with Chabo, on tape, for all the dope he could muster. I wasn't being real shy about my regurgitation. Even if I cared about noise discipline, there was no way to hide the retching. It was a real deep and prolonged heaving that you could've heard a block away. G-Man was very apologetic, thinking I was going to shoot him on the spot, which did cross my mind. He tried to console me that he'd only spit out his old wad of snuff in the drink cup and hadn't used it as a spittoon. Nothing was real helpful to me at that point, although I did manage to get my balaclava up over my face and didn't puke on my raid gear.

In reviewing the taped conversation between Chabo and Elmer, it sounded something like this:

Elmer: I want four pounds of the green (*BLAHHHHHH HA HA HA*) and (*BLAHHHHHH HA HA HA*), six ounces of the other (*BLAHHHHHH HA HA HA*)

Chabo: Is everything all right there?

Elmer: Yeah, someone came over and they are a little sick. (*BLAH HA HA*)

All of the heaving made it onto the tape. Somehow, my peers saw that the recording was made in a digital audio file that was played in the office from time to time, and at my going away party. The last I heard, they were going to try and sell the recording to a morning radio show.

After Elmer gets off the phone, he starts to puke in the garbage can. Just listening to that slug heave made me go again. G-Man was unlucky enough to see Elmer spit up the contents of his stomach and lungs, and ran out the door and into Elmer's apartment to puke in his bathroom. I pulled it together and got my other partners, Ben-jammin and Welche on the Nextel, who were in the apartment, and told them we're having a real good time in the kitchen. All I hear is raucous laughter as Ben-jammin tells me that's what they hear, and that G-Man is losing his lunch in Elmer's commode.

I'm sure they were just laughing with me, and not at me, thinking laughter would be the best medicine. It's nice to have thoughtful friends like that.

Chabo ended up coming through hours later, and sent his girlfriend to the door with four pounds of weed in a shopping bag while he waited in the car. The surveillance/cover team then moved in on Chabo, who lead them on a short foot chase while trying to dump his dope on someone in the local thrift store. It didn't work out well for him. He went into custody, flipped, and the buy busts continued."

Sgt. Aaron Davis, Albany OR Police Dept.

*

QUEEN ESTER

I got to the door expecting a fight,
She opened it up, Good Lord, what a sight!
She stood there, stark naked, being framed by the door,
Everything she had pointed straight at the floor.

I begged her to cover, to which she refused,
Queen insisted on telling me how she'd been used.
Her live-in was out drinking wine all the day,
She decided, when he returned, they would play.

She lay on the couch with her goodies exposed,
Naked as a jaybird, from her head to her toes.
He finally arrived, and started to cook,
Walked by her with nary a look.

"This was just too much," I heard her say,
Grabbed the pan he was using, and swung away.
A large knot formed in the middle of his head,
"*I dozn't wants her charged*" is all that he said.

As I left the house, they were no longer gruff,
But seeing The Queen made me realize *I'm not paid enough*.

Lt. Tom Schulte, Overland MO Police Dept.
(Based on an actual domestic disturbance call)

CONCLUSION

Like a sport highlights segment on ESPN featuring the most pivotal moments of a game one play at a time, this book focused on some of the most prominent aspects of policing, one chapter at a time. It's by no means the authority on any of the topics presented; in fact, entire books have been written in greater detail addressing the issues covered within a single chapter of this book. Instead, it was written to provide a basic understanding of what police work is like, from the sunny-side up to the dirty shoeprints many never see. To gain a better perspective, ask your local law enforcement agency if they offer a ride-along program or a citizen's police academy. Also, take the time to talk to a cop; you'll be surprised at how much they have to say if they know you really want to listen.

Law enforcement is such a unique occupation, that it's difficult to convey an accurate portrayal of the job unless you're actually in the arena experiencing it. There's camaraderie between cops which transcends ordinary friendships, for they share the life and death experiences on the streets outsiders either can't comprehend, or pretend doesn't exist. The bonds forged from their similar experiences draws them close, into a tight brotherhood and sisterhood. Like family, they'll argue and fight among themselves, and at times can't stand being around each other. But despite any personal differences, when it comes to protecting their own, they'll band together and defend one another with all the ferocity of a female grizzly protecting her young cubs.

For whom else would they have to rely on, if not each other?

It takes a unique person to put on the uniform each day and confront the challenges of policing, and while putting themselves in harms way, still possess the compassion to bend down and hug a small child or comfort an elderly person in distress. Though every patrol shift serves up reminders they're fighting a war they can't win, most remain motivated to make a difference whenever possible, for they know if no resistance is given, the darker side of humanity triumphs without a struggle. Indeed, like modern-day shepherds, they have the daunting task of protecting the flock from all the wolves lurking in the shadows.

And make no mistake about it—the wolves are out there, willing to exploit any opportunity to prey on you and your family.

In the introduction, a statement was made that this book may or may not contradict your opinion of those who protect and serve society. Although the final judgment now rests with you, I hope at the very least, you'll view the next officer you encounter through a new set of eyes.

"Blessed are the peacemakers, for they shall be called the children of God." Matthew 5:9 (KJV)

REFERENCES

[1] National Law Enforcement Officers Memorial Fund: *Law Enforcement Officers Killed in the Line of Duty/Past 10 Years (1999-2008).* <http://www.nleomf.com/TheMemorial/Facts/killedlod.htm>

[2] "Force Policies Can Harm Officers," *American Police Beat*, November 2003, pp. 22, 34.

[3] Gavin De Becker, *The Gift of Fear* (Dell Publishing, 1998), p. 38.

[4] "Los Angeles Officer Slain During Domestic Disturbance Call." CalibrePress.Com: Street Survival Newsline # 686. 24 February 2004.

[5] Remsberg, Charles. "Behavior Traits That Get Cops Killed." The Rap Sheet August 2007: A1+. <http://www.portlandpolice association.com/rsissues/Aug07RS2.pdf>

[6] United States. Bureau of Justice Statistics. Intimate Partner Violence Against Women Declined From 1993 Through 1998. 17 May 2000. <http://www.ojp.usdoj.gov/bjs/pub/press/ipv.pr>

7   United States. U.S. Department of Justice: Federal Bureau of Investigation, Criminal Justice Information Services Division. 2007 Law Enforcement Officers Killed and Assaulted. <http://www.fbi.gov/ucr/killed/2007/data/table_68.html>

8   United States. U.S. Department of Justice: Office of Justice Programs, Bureau of Justice Statistics. Intimate Partner Violence, 1993-2001. <http://ojp.usdoj.gov/bjs/abstract/ipv01.htm>

9   "Suicide by Cop." Police Psychology Consultation Center. 2003. <http://www.policepsychconsult.com/suicide.htm>

10   Anglin, Deirdre and H. Range Hutson, et.al. "Suicide by Cop." Annals of Emergency Medicine Dec. 1998: 665+.

11   "Police Work Undermines Cardiovascular Health, Comparison To General Population Shows." Medical News Today. 01 Jul 2009. <http://www.medicalnewstoday.com/articles/156041.php>

www.ingramcontent.com/pod-product-compliance
Lightning Source LLC
Chambersburg PA
CBHW061254280526
45784CB00002B/766